WHISPERS OF A BLEAK DIARY

About the Author:

Hawkar Majeed, a Kurdish author and poet, was born in Kalar and grew up in Hawler. He has authored "Your Knitted Scarf" and co-authored "The Kurdish Progeny" and "High Water". "Whispers of a Bleak Diary" stands as his debut novel. Hawkar was honored by KRI Youth Council" as one of the "Social Media Influencers" in 2019. In his leisure time, he savors long walks in nature, moments of quiet reflection, and journaling in his diary at his preferred café.

Hawkar loves to hear from readers. You can email him at **Hawkar.m.sleman@gmail.com** Other ways to stay in touch with Hawkar:

@hawa_majeed

Hawkar Majeed

@hawkar_majeed

WHISPERS OF A BLEAK DIARY

HAWKAR MAJEED

WHISPERS OF A BLEAK DIARY

Copyright © 2023 Hawkar Majeed

All rights reserved. No parts of this book may be used or reproduced in any manner whatsoever without written permission except in the case of brief quotations embodied in critical articles or reviews.

Cover & Interior Design: **Bassam Mahmoud**
Editor: **Mumin Muhsin**

First Edition, 2023
10 9 8 7 6 5 4 3 2 1

.... Behind these sad spectacles of words, the hope that you might be reading me trembles unspeakably, that I have not completely died in your memory.

Preface:

For several months now, the thought of this book accompanied me constantly. As if something was tossing and turning in me - some wild memories, untimed emotions, and muddled yearnings nagging in my head. Nagging voices craving to find a place where my wounded soul could embrace peace, where my desolate heart could clasp hope in its arm. I know I have regretted writing on many occasions, but what other refuge do I have when an earthquake shakes the coasts and the ocean of my heart, expels its rubble from the depths? When wild waves drive my rusty memories and emotions to the mainland, bringing them from the shipwreck to the surface of the shore and there I am, picking them up one by one, feeling them in my eyes, in my lungs, in my ribs, in my heart, silently in solitude. I admit, it is not me writing down myself, but rather something unfathomable writing me down. This unfathomable force arises somewhere inside, growing from my fears, hopes, dreams, longing, disappointments, and hopelessness, rafting with each other, and becoming like a snow avalanche. I find myself helpless, unable to find refuge from them and hide, their plots themselves pop up in consciousness, regardless of what I am doing or what I think about at the time of their visit. In the end, they are only ethereal and insensitive phantoms that plead only one thing from me - freedom. Freedom from the trap of their place of birth.

Tonight, I finally made up my mind. I absorbed my diary's pages, opened my laptop, went through my phone notes, and found all the drafts from past years. All the poems, letters, prose, and texts never dared to become stories. All those confused memories, caged in the darkness of vanity. I finally typed the first word and let the words spill out. It was not easy. There were tears and shaky breaths, moments of silence, and moments of overwhelming emotion. But with each word I re-wrote, I felt a little bit lighter, like a weight had been lifted off my shoulders. It was as if I had finally allowed myself to exhale after holding my breath for far too long. Embracing my fear, I finally walked up to crown them free rein and allowed them to talk to me - and they started talking. I suddenly noticed a hero; I saw the outlines of his path. I dived into deep thinking to finally see myself fully ready for the birth of a story - the story of this book.

I must admit that I have postponed my "moment" on more than a dozen occasions. And I have been looking with great expectation for the peace that will take all these memories out of my head. I have been hesitant to write this novel and though I am aware of the exact reason, I refuse to accept it, yet it never failed to terrify me. Writing exposes the writer. It is an act of vulnerability, an act of revealing something about a writer to readers. It makes the writer fragile and vulnerable, yet it could simultaneously heal him, too. I am torn between this hope of being healed and the certainty of being vulnerable and fragile. Nevertheless, I am guided by this insane certitude that I must relinquish so that I can receive more, that I must give away as much as possible, to make room for understanding. This is what processing emotions feel like for me. I know in this wild world of mine I may not learn to write well, but I will learn to listen and hopefully understand something. By God, I would have welcomed the possibility of opening my soul through music, drawing, and paintings, but since my childhood life has drowned me in the abyss of words and a whirlpool of texts, where I reveal my truth through the prism of a superb picture. In this abyss I feel warm and tranquil, there is only ink, paper, me, and a whole world of silence.

Finally, I am determined to be candid; I intend to avoid editing and revising this draft more than two times contrary to my habit of editing all the writings I put out there before. I am not going to foolishly try to satisfy my pride and pander to my ego, much less sneak into the feelings of readers in a desperate attempt to look flawless. This time, I write without expectations, I write as the last resort for help that nobody heard. Tired of forcing myself into a box that was too small for me anyway. I will be fearless as I write. I no longer want to resort to distractions, nor play with my creativity to discover that I have lost more than I can in conscience. I know how many nights I have lost over trying to obscure my words with vagueness, and I am aware of how much I lack when I pretend to understand myself.

I want to leave these words which seek no interpretation, nor do they embody a truth, they do not want to decipher a framework in the swamp of self-knowledge, they only try to honor and farewell the feelings and memories. And without much thought, I share them so that whoever receives them can accompany me for a little while.

***

WHISPERS OF A BLEAK DIARY

The morning spread its sunlight and clouds like paint on the window. The city was still wrapped in a slumbering winter haze as the first rays of sunlight filtered through the empty streets. The only sign of life was the warm light pouring out of the open door of a small café, its shelves adorned with books and art. The air was filled with the smooth sounds of jazz, an apt accompaniment to the cozy atmosphere within. Thomas, the barista, with his head against the window glass, placed two fingers on the icy surface of the pane. His head turned slightly towards his hand. His glassy eyes were drawn inward. He lifted one finger, then two, a greasy halo maintaining contact with the glass. He placed his entire palm on it, then removed it. Fine lines crossed these bony shapes, as if canceling them out. He straightened his forehead, caught a glimpse of the same halo that a distant lighthouse brought forth in the blue. From these tiny traces, he knew he was still here. He knew he had not entirely disappeared.

Being an introvert was no easy task, Thomas knew this firsthand. What a misfortune that his work forced him to run into people so often. Sometimes impenetrably stupid, narrow-minded, ignorant, rude people. And worst of all, they did not seem to have heard with their ears and did not read about personal space in reference books. Thomas sometimes wanted to howl in desperation. He could not get rid of people, because he needed them one way or another.

Suddenly, a familiar figure entered the café, a Thirty-one-year-old man in a brown trench coat, flannel trousers, and vintage ankle boots. He was a wanderer looking for a place to belong, who always felt at ease in cafes and found them less intimidating. A traveler's dilemma, I guess, - Perhaps to belong, or to be a temporary person, to be less lonely, too. And in cafes, he could always find a way to connect with others and manage to say a few things.

Thomas greeted him with a welcoming smile as the man sat down at his usual spot by the window and took his usual order, a cappuccino. He had been a regular at the Cafe for quite some time, coming almost every Saturday, regardless of the weather. Thomas and he had a special bond. Many times, they would engage in intriguing conversations. On one of those days, the man poured his heart out to Thomas and told him that he is just a mess wanting to be an art. On another occasion, he revealed to Thomas that often his mind and he do not get along well, that he comes to this cafe only to forget and remember. Just a week ago, he said to Thomas that he has learned to be cautious about whom he risks it all for, in whose hands he places his deepest emotions because not everyone is capable of enduring a wounded soul that suffers silently each day while smiling widely to silence the pain.

Nearly an hour later, a few customers had entered the Café. Around him were groups of huddled people on leathery uneven seats under soft orange lights. There was what appeared to be a first date, a group of old friends, a few older men huddled around emitting bursts of laughter now and again. And another solo individual, with a laptop and pint, click-clacking away at his keyboard. As for the outside world, the city streets were buzzing with more pedestrians.

Pulling out his diary, the man began to write for a good while. Not all cafes can make you a writer, but this one was special. It was a place where he could sit and write, or not write, and still feel like he belonged. Nursing his cappuccino, writing in his diary, looking into space, staring out the window with a distant look in his eyes, he was lost in his world. To be there, waiting, over and over again as the hours pass by, with only a gaze fixed on a point, emptiness, and nothingness. As he wrote, he suddenly felt a sharp pain in his chest. He clutched his chest and gasped for air. He looked around for help, but nobody noticed his agony. The pain became unbearable, he fell to the floor, knocking over his table and scattering his diary and pen. His cappuccino cup fell to the ground, too, shattering into a thousand pieces. Customers and Thomas rushed over to help, but his face was already turning pale. He took his last breath, alone in his favorite café, surrounded by strangers. A hush fell over the café as everyone stood in shock and disbelief. Thomas called for an ambulance, but it was too late. The man had passed away, surrounded by strangers in the cafe he had visited so often.

Thomas noticed the man's diary lying on the floor. Curiosity got the best of him, and he picked it up and the last page of the diary said "For I have suffered a lot from people who walked into my life just to leave their arrows in my heart and watch how I suffer. Familiar faces who left me to my pains, to battle my demons alone, to face my own brokenness." Later that day, Thomas hesitated for a moment, debating whether to leave the intimate musings of the man undisturbed. But the temptation proved too great, and Thomas found himself leafing through the pages that entire night, unable to resist the lure of the man's secrets.

The Man's Diary

To my beautiful Olena,

I have thought and I have wanted to fill your mailbox with letters, but my intention breaks in my hands when I remember that I do not know, not even out of habit, how to write a letter. I lack the aptitude for how to empty my emotions without hiding the metaphors for the purposes of my writing. I regularly hide behind them, hoping, in the most absurd way, to comfort my imagination with a stroke of unreality. Even the fact that I am writing to you in English already falsifies what I wish you to hear me saying and what I want you to understand. The words I use cannot do justice to the depth of my feelings, and they fall short of expressing the love that I hold for you.

For that, I have come to the decision that I am not going to write you letters, but rather I am going to satisfy your curiosity, if you ever had one, with black and white texts and prose, before the questions accumulate, before you despair in waiting. The wait mitigates the nostalgia and convinces me that I live for writing and to remind you that I write for you to read me. To keep present in the fineness of time, that it was you, dear Olena, who led me to shipwreck in the sea of my hopes, in search of a victorious encounter between my confidence and the dream of writing to the world and being read by the corners of the universe. So no, I shall not fill your mailbox with letters, but with sighs, one for each line, one for each memory.

Here is your photo in front of me. Your eyes are looking at me, as if alive. I see the joy and hope in them. When I look into them, I experience an inexplicable feeling of delight and some kind of quiet joy. Yet, for the thousandth time of gazing into your eyes, it feels like pomegranate seeds have been scattered in my heart. It makes me even more restless. It leaves me no choice but to take refuge in the cozy corner of your smile from the sting of the sorrowful laughter that carries loneliness on its lips.

My dear Olena, I know it is six months since the last time I wrote you. Sometimes when I walk in the middle of the crowd, in the very deepest part of my heart, I plead that among all the unknown faces that I usually admire daily, it will be your familiar face once again. Sometimes I try to imagine what you will look like when you are old, and I think I will love you just as much. Maybe even more. I find myself in situations that would connect me to you. Your peculiarities, your interests, your dreams. I take a step back and it takes me a moment to realize that I am missing you less. Yet, it takes me a long while to admit to myself that I do not want to lose you entirely despite the truth that you have been gone for a long time. Perhaps, I have not wholly experienced all of you. Like if I write like you or talk with eloquence like you - that part of you will stay with me forever. No one will be able to take it away from me. After all, I have patched it tightly to my heart and I am not letting go. All the past weeks have passed in thinking. I have been thinking about things that every lover imagines at least once the way they want. I want you to think of them too! I thought about the seagulls flying over Istanbul panorama and Bosporus, about the paddle of the boaters in the dark of Venice nights, about the solitude and silence of watchtower buildings, about the streets of Athens, about you, who gives meaning to time with your five senses, and above all, who amazes me like nothing else. I forgive you for the times I missed you and you were not aware of it. And I forgive myself for waiting for what is no longer expected, what is no longer there and will not come back.

In your absence, I have woven so many stories for you that even if I narrate a thousand and one nights, it would not be enough. It is indeed the world of stories and fantasies that soothe a person in love. Could it be that stories are the wings that allow us to fly toward our imagination? I also have hundreds of unfinished poetry lines that keep the echo of your name in their verses. Poems that you will never read, that you will never hear, that you will never feel. You know too well that poems are my only way of saying goodbye and thus trying to soften my feelings towards you because even though it is all over, there are still fragments of you in my heart. I shall therefore keep writing these lines, for behind these sad spectacles of words, a hope that you might be reading me trembles unspeakably, that I have not completely died in your memory. This hope quivers within me, unspeakable in its intensity, like the fluttering of a fragile butterfly's wings. I plead and ask you to read me. Read me between the lines and reply with written notes about the minutes. Minutes that reach me and soothe sadness at night and ask me —What does it feel like to be loved? Write to me please, I know you are a writer because you think like a writer. Because you try to store the things that happen to you, because you remember people's names, places, plots, because you have a tendency to recall the past in the form of stories, because you do not just live experiences, but you want to analyze them in search of a beginning, a development, and an end, because through writing you make sense of things. Write to me about the sky, the sea, the stars, the sunset, the beauty, the dreams, and most importantly, write to me about yourself. I want to see the world through your eyes, I want to see you through your writings. You have no idea how few simple words about your well-being can change my colorless and silent world.

And read me between the lines and find all the words I never dared to pronounce. Unlock the silences that have guarded my heart and find the key that I revealed to you every day between glances, to understand why I have loved you so stealthily, why I have not been able to prove it, or why I have hidden it under my tongue when speaking. Read me about the brilliance of our memories and hum to me one of those songs that only your lips know how to hum, sing me one of those backward ballads that your imagination invents, and dedicate your whistles to me from one corner of the room to another. Read me for all the time I have dedicated to you in secret and discover that I no longer write for another more noble reason than to remember you among my writings.

***

Barcelona, February 22, 2020

Who am I in this fragile world? Am I an unwanted child? A lonely wanderer? A suffering lover? A lost traveler? Tales of personality? Or just an abundance of cells? These thoughts haunt me every time I think about the world around me. As if everything that exists in the world cannot exist separately. This realization hits me hard, causing me to freeze again and avert my gaze from the people around me. My thoughts are confused, stumbling against each other. Thousands of me are within me, each one tearing apart the other. The voices dissolve before they reach me as if falling before my inner chaos. A cool and salty wind kisses my cheeks, leaving its imperceptible mark, trying to attract attention.

The sun slowly sets on the horizon, casting a warm, golden glow across the sandy shore of Barcelona Beach. The salty sea air fills my lungs, invigorating me with its freshness and brine. The crystal-clear waters of the Mediterranean Sea stretch out to the horizon, sparkling and inviting, I hear the distant cries of seagulls and the gentle sound of waves lapping at the shore, creating an enchanting rhythm that fills me with a sense of serenity. The sky is painted in shades of pink and orange, with streaks of violet and gold thrown in for good measure. Such a heavenly picture has not touched my heart for a long time.

There is a sense of tranquility that envelops me as I walk, a stillness that is only broken by the occasional cry of a seagull or the soft rustle of the wind. The world seems to slow down. Inhaling the smell of the sea with a full chest, I feel the anguish that lulls my vigilance and common sense. I take a step toward the gray waves; I take the second. My eyes are riveted by only one picture: the sea is washed ashore, washing away everything nearby. Although the waves are small, they would not have reached, in my opinion, even the ankles, they still seem so serious and angry. I like how the warm sea takes me into the abyss of cold and endless darkness. A sad sound escapes from within. It flies away too fast, like a broken string that decides to run away. And it is sad even to imagine these futile attempts to escape from the cold instrument to which it is tied at one end, like a dog to a booth. Sometimes I feel like that string!

I lift my foot and gently place my sandal on the wet sand. Pushing it back, I examine the patterns of the sole. Whimsical lines are softly carved on a dark surface. Their life is noticeably short. The wave covers my trail as if I were not here. I bite my lower lip, tilt my head to the side and realize the saddest and most incomprehensible thought: I have the same thing with memory. Waves unevenly wash away everything around: somewhere more, somewhere less. I take a small step to the side, make footprints, and find a point where the waves can never reach my trail.

I squat down in front of this very point of contact and put my head on my shoulder. It hurts me terribly the realization that this trace, like you, is in my memory. It seems like I can forget my own birthday, my friends' names, and my best friend's favorite songs, but you… this connectedness to you is eternal, this attachment to you is undying. The waves will never reach all that is indicated by your name and velvety voice. I must drown in these footprints. I desperately clutch at the air with my hands, trying to say everything - if only not to lose these memories. And who would not say that it is useless, that you will not return, and the thoughts are so real and intrusive? And the world is so small, where every element is part of one whole.

For a moment I bury my nose in my knees, smelling the sun, inhale the insipid smell, and get up. A slight dizziness from harshness has already become normal and habitual, and I do not even understand how you can do without it. The world stops spinning and it is getting dark, my eyes settled on the colors of the sky. Everything begins to darken, reminding me of the coming twilight. Carefully move to the sand, where I cannot see the little stars, The world around me is changing gradually, but noticeably for me. Examining what is happening on the horizon and under my feet, I can understand how everything around me is petty and hopeless. This causes melancholy. I close my eyes sharply, gritting my teeth. The wind keeps calling me to the dark and deep sea. It seems that with a little more try, she might persuade me. Shaking my head, I open my eyes, turn around and walk slowly across the sand. Sandals fall through, scooping up grains of sand. I usually hate this feeling. Looking at how the grains roll down, kissing my fingers, I again do not perceive the people who, for some reason, crowded around the shore.

Exactly... Shore... Sometimes the shore becomes the safest ear to hear your whispers. And when you come in peace, the first wave hides all your secrets in the heart of the sea until the curious and drowsy sun's first rays.

I look back at you for the last time to see the subtle curves of the sole, and... My tear-filled eyes widen. My chest tightens so hard that it becomes difficult to breathe, and my legs suddenly buckle sharply. The waves washed away the last traces that reminded me of someone I should never forget.

But who? ... whom was I talking about?

***

As the morning light creeps through the windows of my cold, stone-walled room, I smile to myself. Always, after a night of rest, I wake up happy and refreshed, the deep vitality renewed. Another day! I feel an overwhelming urge to write. I want to write down every detail about you, about us, about what we were and what we could have been. I want to capture the sea that separates us and the sky that unites us. I want to speak of sleepless nights and shared dreams. I want to write about the love I feel and the fear that invades me. But my diary lies forgotten on the desk, its empty pages mocking me with their perfection, and suddenly a wave of emotions sweeps over me, only to realize that I am struggling to keep my emotions stable lately.

Sometimes I have a hard time putting a name to my feelings. In the mornings, I feel content and hopeful, but as the day wears on, a sense of despair overcomes me for no apparent reason. My sorrow is not my own, it stems from the tales of others that have found their way to me. It clutches me with an icy grip, leaving no space for solace. Their fleeting feelings are difficult to express in words, much like the inability to look at oneself in the mirror when overwhelmed by emotions. And even if I were to attempt to document these shifts, I fear my words would fall short of capturing their true essence.

Recently, my inbox has become a sea of messages. The same old tune - lost souls seeking refuge in my words, pouring their hearts out to me. They tell me that they understand my writing, that my emotions make sense to them, that they too are writers or dream of becoming one but are stuck in monotonous jobs or a life that crush their souls. They write to me that they do not always have the patience for crowds, nor do they have patience to constantly isolate themselves and enjoy loneliness! Some nights, they like to be in a group of fifteen or twenty people and laugh so much that they do not realize when morning comes! And sometimes they want to turn off their phones and spend a few hours alone with themselves! The silence of their apartments crushes them. They cannot stand being alone in their room with only their thoughts for company, and they desperately need someone to talk to. Yet they are the most beautiful souls who swallow their pain and avoid letting others taste it. They tell me that they go from wanting to feel something to not wanting to feel anything at all. They write to me that they want to fall in love, to feel the butterflies in their stomach, the sparks, to laugh with someone until tears, to take aimless drives until late at night. They say they want to experience something outside of their apathy.

They believe I have the words that can soothe their pain, that I possess the magical formula for curing loneliness. But the truth is, I am just as lost and alone as they are. Sometimes, after each message, I collapse in despair, I double over in my room and mutter "For God's sake" to myself, feeling overwhelmed by the despair that permeates our world. The loveless people, the empty streets, the suffocating loneliness, the walls that close in on us— all of it is my reality too. They think I am holding back some secret, but the truth is, I do not write out of knowledge. I write because I am searching for answers just like they are. I write to save myself from plunging into the bottomless pit of madness, I write to bare my soul onto the page, unleashing the demons within so they may not enslave me, just like these lost souls intend.

After answering each message, I get tired and I yearn for someone to offer me the words that could ease my pain, just as those messages in my inbox do. Sometimes I suffer moments of regret and remorse for expressing my words, and my heart remains heavy. Sometimes I feel like wherever I step, there is no trace of me. Nobody even thinks of me anymore. Occasionally, someone remembers me by name or the scent of a fragrance, but quickly changes the subject as I become a burden on the atmosphere. Neither the earth, nor the moon and sun, nor any star or galaxy has changed for me. All are following their own plans and spending their time. Nobody knows my favorite color, what my favorite song means to me, what flower I like, or what I think about certain topics. I am tired of pretending that it is enough that they only know my birthday. Sometimes I cry distantly for the other "I am" in me, the escaped one in my blood, the hopeful, the adventurer who left at night to chase the sad faces that his sick desire presented to him. I pray that perhaps in another universe, there is a brave version of me, realizing his dreams and with the girl he loves by his side. Maybe he is stable, perhaps he is stronger and does not let anyone dull his brilliance. He is everything I have ever wanted, and I constantly ask myself, "Will I ever be able to traverse all the universes to reach him?".

The clocks continue to rotate in all cities, homes, and streets, indifferent to our moments. I go back to listening to Bach – I go back to smelling the soil of the garden – I go back to thinking of poems and novels – I go back to the silence that makes a rainy morning the beginning of the world of tomorrow. I open my heart toward more of those screams, pains, and cries in my inbox and turn it into a graveyard of many stories and dreams, a place where the lost and lonely can come to find refuge, a beacon of hope for those who are searching for a way out of the abyss.

***

Wrocław, October 10, 2019

As I was delving into the pages of my old diary, one occasion stole my attention. A conversation that seems I once had with a little girl in one of the local bookstores.

"What does it mean to be a writer?"

asks the little girl in whose eyes I saw nothing but fear and restlessness.

"To be a writer is to be a soldier caught in the culmination of a battle with nothing but a sheet of paper and a pen," I reply.

"While spears and arrows tear the air, while the cries of the wounded swirl with the dust, you are struck by an invisible arrow. You bleed blue blood that flows from the tip of your nib. All your pain, suffering, apathy, and even that little bit of euphoria, leave bloody traces on that paper. Those traces of blood going to reincarnate into prose and lyrics that will come out of your born soul." I continue, "I say start, my friend because to be a writer you have to have a wound from which to draw your ink. You are one of the greatest artists whose works will feed the souls destitute for love, which will drink the youth parched for empathy."

"Have we succeeded so far?", the girl's voice trembles.

"Yes, we have!"

I tell her through the tears that blur my vision, while the mirror in front of me breaks into millions of pieces.

After reading this, anxious anticipation threatened to clutter my inner space with a black wave. Only writing can save. The beginning of a new story. Everything is mixed in it: mysticism, fantasy, dystopia. I am interested in writing about people, their fears, their hope, their pain, their joy, their faith, and their disbelief. For I believe that there is no greater relief than discovering a book that talks about your tormenting and communes to the deepest parts of your soul, a comfort in knowing that someone out there understands the turmoil within you, a story that makes you feel seen, a reminder that you are not alone in your struggles. And if my writing could bring that kind of solace to just one person, then I know it would all be worth it. But I also write to survive. Words are my food, my oxygen, my water, the light of my day, chastely awaited, like a thirsty wanderer in a desert. They enter through my skin, poison my blood, and haunt my soul. Verses have replaced my blood vessels, they flow through the ages of sung love, suffering, sadness, and even happiness. My heart, once flesh and blood, has rotted away - replaced it with poetry. Minute by minute she pumps melancholy lyrics that echo through this temple I call my body. I cultivate that temple, that shelter, every day with the sun, I tend to it lovingly, and I water it with an unending flow of words. I love to be able to write, to be able to show the world my blood woven into words, my soul sewn into the pages of books.

I love to craft stories, weave prose, feel the fate of my characters, and see words come out under my fingers as if I am but a humble guide between the real and the fictional world. Being a writer is to live in two worlds: the world of everyday, with its mundane routines and obligations, and the world of the imagination, where anything is possible. It is to be both observer and participant, to look upon the world with a critical eye, yet to be open to the beauty and wonder that surrounds us, a fleeting expression, a ray of sunlight on a dewy morning, the sound of laughter in the distance. It is to see the beauty in the mundane and to find meaning in the smallest of moments.

To be a writer is to live a life of curiosity and wonder, a life of introspection, of constantly questioning and exploring the self. Writing is a journey between the past and the future guided by the present. It is a journey into the past, a quest to recapture the memories and emotions of bygone days. It is to evoke the sights, sounds, and smells of a world that may no longer exist, to offer a glimpse into a world that is at once familiar and strange. At times, being a writer can be a solitary and isolating experience. It is often a struggle to find the right words, to craft a sentence or a paragraph that truly captures what we want to say. Yet, it is also a journey of connection, a way to touch the hearts and minds of others, to share vulnerability and life stories to create bridges.

***

I loved our deep conversation last night, it ignited a flame within me, a passion that consumed every fiber of my being. My heart desired to remain there, in those moments, where you brought me love. And with a thread of glances, you closed some old wounds of mine, something within me started to ignite a fire that glowed and burned with raw power with every glance exchanged. I was not sure I could wield it, but I had to give it a try. Last night, though my heart raced twice as fast, a smile appeared on my face, the feeling that I was alive again. In my soul, there was a celebration of the sun. I wanted to chat about the stars, about silly things in the past, about what I loved, about the weather, about everything... about all those impossible things.

I loved how we almost went through everything in our lives in less than ten minutes. I loved how you turned that crisp winter night into the warmest one of all my time. I loved how you made me forget about sad songs and have a wild smile on my face all the next day. Oh, how I yearned for the clock to falter, for time to relinquish its relentless grip, granting us an eternity to bask in each other's presence. I wished the night would stretch its silken embrace, allowing us the luxury of more stolen moments, more stolen glances. I wished the night was long and you had more time to stay.

Maybe another night, maybe another day. For I want to listen to you again, to listen to your stories, I am very eager to read your writings, to feel your feelings, and see how you felt in those moments of life. Let me gaze at you. In the metro, on the road, on the pedestrian bridge, and on the sidewalk, let me stare at you and not blink. When you cautiously bring your lips closer to the white cup, lest the heat of the coffee scorches them. Let me examine you more closely, your smile and frown. Your tiny eyes when they concentrate and the detached gaze when you are lost in a dream. I do not know if I will be alive or dead tomorrow. Just sit; let me look at you with my heart. Maybe we can meet again, very soon, at a nearby café so that we talk more about our lives. Let is turn all these "maybes" into "finally". Let's meet the dawn on the roof of the nine-story building. We will sit wrapped in one blanket. Nearby there will be mugs of tea, from which warm steam will come, in this early still cool morning, but the sky will already be slightly filled with light.

***

Wroclaw, November 2, 2019

Nestled in the heart of Wroclaw, there is a place where coffee and literature are celebrated equally. It is a café and bookstore called Café Księgarnia Tajne Komplety, a hidden gem tucked away in a quiet corner, with its bright orange sign standing out against the surrounding buildings. As I pushed open the door, the warm, inviting atmosphere and the aroma of freshly brewed coffee enveloped me, but beneath the surface, I could sense something more. Soft jazz music drifted through the air, creating an eerie, otherworldly ambiance that sent chills down my spine. The shelves lining the walls were filled with books and magazines, each one seeming to hold its own mysterious secrets. The barista greeted me with a friendly smile, I went to her, and I ordered a cappuccino, marveling at the way she meticulously crafted the perfect cup.

The Café was decorated with vintage furniture, plush armchairs, and cozy reading nooks. The walls were adorned with artwork and shelves of books, inviting customers to relax and linger. I could not resist browsing the selection of books for sale. From classic novels to contemporary bestsellers, the shelves were filled with a wide variety of titles, each one beckoning me to explore its pages. I lost track of time in the cozy confines of Księgarnia Tajne, savoring each sip of my cappuccino and devouring each page of my book. I lost myself in the pages of the poetry collection, feeling as if I had found a kindred spirit in the words. I felt as though I had been transported to a different world, one where the only thing that mattered was the warmth of the cafe and the beauty of the words on the page. It was as if I had stumbled upon a treasure trove of hidden gems, waiting to be discovered. Around me, the sounds of soft conversation and the rustling of pages filled the air while the sounds of the city faded away. Particles of dust hover in the rays of the sun, and the aroma of old books envelops every nook and cranny here. If you find yourself drawn to this place by chance, know that fate itself has led you here and that you are always welcome. Many books are waiting for you on the shelves, dreaming that you will read them.

I savored the last sip of my frothy cappuccino, letting the warmth of the mug seep into my palms as I turned my attention to the book in my lap. I let my gaze wander over the pages of the book, the words blurring as my thoughts turned to her.

I knew that this little corner cafe was a haven of cozy charm where we could sink into plush armchairs and lose ourselves in conversation. With a sense of excitement, I pulled out my phone and composed a message to her, inviting her to meet me at Księgarnia Tajne. I described the space, the vintage furniture, the plush armchairs, and the inviting reading nooks. As I hit send, I felt a flutter of anticipation in my chest. Little did I know that this quaint little bookshop would become the heart and soul of our "room to read" club. A place where we poured our hearts and souls into our writings, sharing our insights and discussing literary works of old and new. A corner where she would introduce me to the music works of Frédéric Chopin and I would introduce her to the voice of Leonard Cohen.

Moments later, my phone buzzed with her message, and I felt a rush of excitement, she was on her way. Sitting in a corner, the dog of the owner's café lay curled up at my feet. I gazed out the window, sipping on a warm cup of coffee. Suddenly, the door opened, and she walked in, the person who made my heart flutter with joy. Her eyes sparkled in the soft light of the Café as she made her way towards me. Our eyes met, I left the shy roses on my cheeks in her eyes and got myself lost in her presence, like a wandering moon over the waves, then surrendered too quickly to the pull of her gaze. Ten thousand possibilities spoken in a second mute of runaway heartbeats. We settled into the plush armchairs, our hands wrapped around our cups as we shared stories and laughter. As we stepped into the dance of souls, exchanging emotions and essences, we stood before the thundering beach of that café. The dim light only intensified the moment, as our confidence remained unshaken by the crashing waves.

The afternoon flew by in a blur of warmth and connection. We lingered for a while, lost in conversation and the comforting ambiance of Księgarnia Tajne. As the time of departure drew near, a feeling of melancholy washed over me. It was not just the thought of saying goodbye to her and this enchanting evening, but the realization that I was leaving behind a piece of myself in this place and time, a part that I would never get back. We walked back to her apartment. At the doorstep, bid each other "good night" and "See you tomorrow in class". The lyrics of Frank Sinatra's "Strangers in the Night" lingered in my mind as we exchanged our parting words. I felt like we both felt the same thing, it was that feeling when you realize that if you do not do something now, it will probably be the biggest regret of your life, a constant pain in your heart that will stay with you forever. Yet, our eyes locked for one last time, but our hearts were content with silence. We shared a smile, knowing that sometimes words fall short of expressing what we truly feel.

***

She sadly lowers her head, propping it up with her hand. And she looks into the distance, but as if through time. She delves into the past, each time trying to find something that would give her peace. Something that would heal her wounds. And then move on. But life keeps pushing her forward, hitting her in the back harder and harder.

"Sometimes the world does not need saving."

She looks at me with interest, waiting for an explanation. She cannot read my thoughts, and my words too often come in riddles. "He's old enough to take care of himself," I say inadvertently. "The only ones who need saving are ourselves."

She does not say anything. She thinks over my words for a few minutes and then nods - as if to herself. She takes my words to heart, but it is hard for her to sigh.

"Promise me that one day I will not have to save you."

And the words hit hard, like a mirror shattering into pieces. They make me scared, my heart shrinks in my chest... It is the feeling when you are caught off guard, but there is nowhere to run and hide. And where could I hide from her gaze of violet eyes that make me want to live?

My hand reaches for the prayer beads on my neck. It is an ordinary prayer beads from my father; my mother gave it to me a few days after his death - it contains all the magic of his soul, but it has a crack. And every day it grows even deeper, penetrating inside.

"I promise." She finally speaks.

With a tender gesture, she leans towards me, resting her head gently upon my shoulders.

"What do you fear most in the world?" The question sounded soft and gentle, as if she is afraid to scare me away. And I do not know what to answer, so I avert my gaze and cling to the grass swaying in the wind.

She does not rush me, only waits patiently, giving me as much time as I could not have carried away in a century. And the silence is too tense. In one beautiful moment, a word slips from my lips, that I never expected to hear:

"Losing you"… And thunder rumbles across the sky.

***

Wroclaw, November 4, 2019

For years now, I have kept my dark thoughts to myself, burying them deep inside my mind where nobody could see them. There were moments when I forced a smile to hold back tears. For that, I am now a graveyard of dark thoughts and sad memories and I do not wish to burden anyone with the weight of my inner struggles. So instead, I put on a brave face and soldier on. But as time goes on, the weight of these thoughts becomes unbearable. They are like a heavy anchor dragging me down, pulling me deeper and deeper into a place of darkness and despair.

I am haunted by the regret of not knowing how to deal with myself sometimes, it pains me to admit that at times I struggle to exhibit the delicate, empathetic touch that is expected of me. It is indeed a source of great sorrow to know that I cannot simply turn away from those who inflict pain upon me. The weight of their presence in my life is often suffocating, and I feel as though I am but a mere shadow in their world. I despise my own weakness, the ease with which I am brought to tears, and the wounds that cut me to the bone. On those days, I push away those closest to me by retreating into myself, and the guilt that follows is all-consuming. In moments like these, I feel as though the universe is conspiring against me, and that my own powerlessness is overwhelming. But I know that these thoughts must be endured, weathered like the changing of the seasons, or released along with the tears that come with them. But what do I really know about healing? Because I know of cold fears that hide under my chest to make winter nights warmer, I know of sad songs to make wounds comfortable when the hours go by burning without a plan. I know more about death than life, but I blame life for not knowing how to teach; I know about birds at three in the morning, when I cannot sleep, let alone dream, I know about hate, a little malpractice in love, and melancholy.

I know if I do not handle my thoughts on time, I will regret it and I will be consumed by them. But how? How can I ever stop and escape from them when I have long been immersed in vanity and have not written a word for a long time out of fear? I see there are countless thoughts pouring and pouring onto the paper of my timeworn diary and it seems that just about it, overflowing and choking, as if the ink itself struggles to keep up. And when the last page is filled with a chaotic tangle of illegible scribbles, my fingers race to capture the images that swirl in my head. I know the key to unlocking my innermost thoughts lies in the unrestrained flow of emotion that flows through me. I strive to write in the moment, to capture the very heartbeat of life itself, to write without hesitation or concern for style, and without waiting for the perfect moment or place. It is the process that matters. I seize whatever is within reach - be it a scrap of paper, a doorstep, or a desk - and write feverishly. By writing at the instant, I capture the rawest form of life's rhythm. Nothing can halt the flow of words once they start pouring out, and at that moment, I ride the wild wave of inspiration to the depths of my creativity. For I believe beauty lies not in the finished product's polish, but in the unfiltered expression of the soul. It is for this madness that my diary is now woven from small pieces of one whole story. I am sure that someday they will come together to form a real book. I would very much like the world to hear my story.

Lately, I find myself weighed down by a heavy load of useless thoughts and ideas that I long to shed. I yearn to unlearn the pointless concepts that have cluttered my mind so that I can rediscover my true self and authentic intentions. I refuse to succumb to the conformist norms that ensnare us all in a collective whole that fits nobody. Everywhere I turn, I see people moving in groups, like schools of fish, and this is one of my greatest fears. I despise the idea of conformity and mediocrity. With unwavering conviction, I am committed to staying true to my innermost self, unburdened by any facades or artifice. The person within me deserves nothing less than my authentic expression, free from any pretense or game-playing. It is my sincerest endeavor to refrain from deceiving not only myself but also those around me. Yet, I cannot help but ponder - is it too great a request to make of myself? Will the world ever understand the depths to which I must go to uphold this oath to myself?

As I am sitting in my room, observing this world, I cannot help but feel a disconnect. The sights and sounds around me are like a movie playing out before my eyes, and I am merely a spectator. I would rather document it all with pen and paper, capturing each moment in ink rather than living it out. And when I am not writing, I immerse myself in playing my guitar, letting the notes carry me away to a world beyond this one. I wander the aisles of bookstores, taking in the knowledge and stories within each cover.

And as I watch the humans bustling around me, I feel content in my solitude. I remind myself that there is no safer destination than the corner of solitude. For in my writing, in my book reading, in my daily walks, in my guitar playing, I find a sanctuary that this world cannot offer.

***

To Olena Petrovych,

And here we are at the end of December. Through the window of my cold dormitory room, I see a man, standing in the nearby train station. His heart is filled with despair, and he wants to bid farewell. He wants to say goodbye to those who turned his life into a living hell. At the end of this very December, there is a lady on the bridge of this city, who looks down the bridge to see the reflection of the moon in the river below, clutches onto the happy odd moments of her life, and wishes that the new year brings more of them into her heart. And as for me, I stay awake in my dormitory room on these December nights. Every night insomnia walks into my room and steals sleep from my eyes. Then drags me into strife with myself. I start drawing a portrait of you in the form of poetry to forget about the strife. I draw your eyes, your face, I draw your smile. looking for a bit of warmth to overcome my cold room for a while.

In your previous letter, you wrote to me about the apple orchard near your house in Ukraine, and I am eager to take a walk there. There is an old myth that says God used to bury hidden secrets in apple orchards. I wish that one day we could bury the secret of our love in that orchard, among the soil. Perhaps our love story will also change the course of creation. You know how red apples can tempt a person! As for now, please, behold the trees swaying gently in the breeze, the stones reflecting in the polished water, the sky with the whisper of stars, the water with its delightful melody, the red tulips in the expanse of green plains, and my heart amidst the abundance of your love. How can it become even more beautiful? By God, remember that He breathed this wondrous magic into our souls so that an indissoluble bond would be between us, my beloved. I swear I have never been so joyful, and I have never seen the world so beautiful, except now when my heart is enveloped by your love. Believe me, God also wants us to be in love, otherwise, the wind would not treat the trees in a way you described in your letter.

I miss you; I miss the heartbeats and the silence your presence used to create. I miss the way the sky presented itself when you were around the corner of our university. I miss the way the lights of the sun used to wave through tree leaves when you were smiling radiantly. I miss you, like someone misses air as he is dragged down in the ocean, gasping for breath. How can I ignore you when with every look of yours, thousands of love flames ignite within me, and each time I see you, it intensifies all my profound emotions? I am devoted to you. I plead that you never accuse me of ignoring you. I see you in dreams, in wakefulness, in reverie, in emptiness, and even in non-existence, for I believe my eyes have been created solely to behold you.

When you come back from your charismas holiday, I want to turn every cafe, museum, cinema, park, and street in the world into a loving memory with you right when come back to Wroclaw. I plan to wander around all the cities with you, telling you jokes and making you laugh, helping you forget the tiredness of the road. I dream to read to you all the love poems, classical ones, and contemporary ones. I want to read to you all the novels, all the books we buy in the bookstores on our way. I want to get lost in every moment of life with you, bad and good moments of life. I want to laugh, to cry, to say no words, to jump, to run, to dance for no particular reason at all, I want to do them all with you and for you. I want to live in a world of wonderful wanderings with you, a world where each breath is a gasp, each sound a scream, each touch a burn, yet we keep moving. And yes, I dream about wood crackling in the fireplace, a warm blanket, and you next to me.

***

She said, "Hate is a very strong word, do not you think?".

"Love is too." I replied.

Looking into her eyes, I then add "Yet people talk about it like it does not mean anything. Ask yourself this question, how can biology or logic possibly explain or understand the physical pain lovers feel in their chests when all they want to do is to be with their beloved? That psychic knife into their souls, how can we ever understand it?".

***

Sometimes the rage of emotions which I am going through is too complicated to be digested with logic and reasoning, and too heavy on my poor heart to overcome with the words of songs or cups of coffee or early sleep. Sometimes it is hard to describe the feelings that linger on a nerve in my body. They fight each other, completely contradictory, sometimes driving me to the edge of despair and other times to the madness of euphoria. Sometimes both states happen at the same time no matter how ridiculous it sounds. Like a tree stump, there on a dune. Dry as hell with no life and yet still stuck in beauty and resisting the wind. Sometimes these feelings take the form of desolate emptiness, a void that seems impossible to fill. Sometimes it is beautiful, saturated with nostalgia, evoking a cascade of tears from my eyes.

I know I am nothing but a shattered soul, shattered beyond repair and I do not dare to call myself anything else than that. For that, I must write to find release from the surge of these emotions I feel. This journey of writing takes me to places I have never been, seen, or heard of. But I find it is the truth of who I am. My beloved resides within me, in between the spaces of my heartbeat, when these moments are felt they turn into poetry. I find it can be terrifying sometimes, my mind can run away into bad places and scary worries. It is not easy to live with such a shadow, especially in this era, in a time of a cult of joy, motivation, and a forced optimistic attitude. Sometimes I feel like every thread, every thought that comes into my head momentarily begins a fight with some weird side of my personality. This quirky side crushes every argument, diminishes every joy, and degrades every moment of delight to the next whimper of conscience. The ejection is always based on the same foundation. That I am not enough in everything. Not good enough to deserve praise, not bad enough to deserve reproach, not tired enough to be happy, not demanding enough to be admired. I think one word that defines me is: ephemeral. A sentence that could better define me would be: "Stray bullet has more direction than me". I have grown accustomed to handling everything alone, like a lone wolf.

Bombarding myself with throwbacks, I am under constant fire. My thoughts are often dark, like tar lumps, they have blocked the exit to the light. I think my intrusive thoughts are starting to create a reality where I cease to exist. The pain ceased to exist for me as a concept, but not as a distant feeling. A feeling that swoops in without warning, without knocking, without asking. It just settles in my living room, waits for me to come home, and follows me around like an annoying fly until I finally pay attention to it. I admit that it is there, and its presence annoys me.

For all of that, pardon me, if sometimes I refrain from speaking too much on the phone or if you see me at a loss for words every time we meet. It is because I have lots of noise in my head. On some days it goes on for an hour, sometimes it goes on for days. It feels like weight-bearing me down. I wish there was like a button or something so that I could turn off my head those times. And if you ask what my soul looks like, then please know it is sometimes twisted and torn, lost, entwined. Sometimes, a glitter, a little light, a bright radiant light. Some days a colorful rainbow inside a forest with long trees and a waterfall but also thunder inside a hurricane. Some days the sparkle of sunshine shimmers on the water but also a fragile flower vase. Yet often, it is a shapeless void, like the shadow of a flame.

I try to be optimistic; I swear, I do. I try to think that this whole thing is not as bad as it seems. I am acting up again, I tell myself, but the reality is that the last time I felt ecstatic and believable happiness was years ago. Now, I feel a deep-sea solitude, to be more specific: the solitude of a narrow, dark, underwater cave. It is no use screaming because no one will hear. I am starting to lose my energy to think. It is wearing me out. I am floating in an icy, claustrophobic abyss. Is there absolution? Is there poetry? Will I ever see the bright morning light again? I do not know. I just wish I was not so... so alone. There is a big difference between willingly wanting to be alone and the one who is left behind alone.

Many people say that I am like autumn. Enchanting and inspired, sometimes sad and tired, but soulful and warm. And perhaps that is true, but one thing to know: I am often consumed by my own thoughts. I am often eaten up by my own fears. And not everything from this can be overcome.

What more should I write for you to understand? The story has already been told. I already know everything. Life like dew is drying out beautifully, and peacefully. Instead of counting down the weeks, I am counting down the glasses. Instead of choosing a closet for the hall, I chose a coffin.

***

Wroclaw, January 15, 2020

As I wandered through the charming streets of Wroclaw, I could not help but feel that I was on the cusp of something truly magical. I caught glimpses of couples holding hands and stealing kisses, lost in their own world of love and creating memories. The city seemed to be a place where love could bloom, where two hearts could find each other amidst the chaos of life. And then I saw her – my dearest Olena, a vision of beauty and grace, with eyes as blue as the Danube and hair as gold as gold could go, walking towards me with a smile on her face. Her smile was like the sun breaking through the clouds, and I felt a surge of something warm and electric inside of me. Our eyes met, our hearts danced to the rhythm of the city, and I felt a jolt of electricity pass between us. She ignites a spark within me. She leaves many, many words in my silent world. Many, but not nearly enough. She speaks to my soul without breathing, without even knowing it. She awakens such a longing in me that I want to speak. To scream, without fear, without thinking about every word, every glance. And as long as this longing exists within me, perhaps a very small part of her will continue to exist through my words.

At that moment, I knew that she was the one, the person I had been searching for. I knew that I had found the missing piece of my soul. Suddenly, "I was not alone" echoed in my head, for beside me walked the one who had captured my heart. I could not help but be drawn to her, with skin like ivory and hair like golden silk, and her eyes were deep pools of mystery. There was something about her that radiated warmth and intelligence, a combination that was impossible to resist. We met in October in this city, amidst the grandeur of its architecture and the hum of its bustling streets. In the heart of Wroclaw, beneath the soft glow of the streetlights, a love story unfolded. It was a tale of two souls, entwined by fate, and drawn together by an unspoken bond. There was an instant connection between us, a feeling of familiarity that made it seem as though we had known each other for a lifetime. It was as though fate had brought us together, two strangers in a city full of endless possibilities.

As the day turned into evening, we strolled along the banks of the Odra River. We sat together by the river, watching the sunset. The city lit up around us, casting a warm glow over everything and everyone. The world, the city, and the wind whispered to me "You have found your home, your soulmate, your life friend." Yes.... I sure did.... Because after so many disappointments, she arrived, and my soul felt at peace all of a sudden. Every street corner, every hidden alleyway, held a memory of our time together. The scent of fresh pastries from a nearby bakery, the sound of church bells ringing in the distance, and the warmth of the sun were on our faces as we sat in a quiet park. She was ordinary and she loved pink sunsets, night cities, and the beauty of the starry sky. She saw beauty even where there was none, and she lived here and now. I knew I would always carry a piece of Wroclaw with me - the memories of the girl who made me fall in love with this city, and the hope that one day, we might be reunited again.

***

We were riding a train in an unknown direction, trying to run away as far as possible. You were looking out the window, at the landscapes that were changing one after another, and you looked so thoughtful. You always look so thoughtful when you gaze into the distance.

And then everything suddenly changes. A smile blossoms on your face. You turn to me, pointing to something far away, noticing, telling me about it, and I cannot take my eyes off of you. You smile sincerely, warmly...and a little bit amusingly, because with your smile, you squint your eyes so cutely.

You fall asleep when several hours pass on the journey. The road was not at all close. I cover you with a blanket, tuck strands of hair behind your ear. And you are like a little sun. Beautiful and cute, sleeping with your mouth slightly open...I look at you and understand... it could not have been anyone else, ever.

Because I love you ... And if you ever doubt love, just try to feel mine.

***

Wroclaw, 2020

The night is an uninvited guest, outside the window of my room, somewhere high above the roofs of my dormitory, the moon hangs, immersed in soft clouds. The tulle is slightly swaying from the cold wind that wanders through the open window, and lofi hip-hop is quietly playing in the dormitory. Walking the endless field of my memories alone is the thing that hurts and aches the most. It is hard and it is very lonely. Especially when you are the only one staring at the gaping abyss of what was, then, and what is, now.

My thoughts always wander back to my dad. He haunts me with his absence. I am yearning hourly and looking for his eyes in a crowd of strangers. I see it in the frames of old films, in the smell of other people's perfumes, in the sounds of music from random playlists, in the lines of books of classical literature, in the poems of twentieth-century poets, in raindrops and the first snowflakes. I keep looking. I hope he wants to meet me. It is the flame of this longing that intensifies and stirs the whirlpool of my heart to rise, and overflow from the windows of my eyes. It causes me this madness you see in me. My heart has become a rose. I am enamored by its heavenly fragrance. Sometimes I feel like a leaf, shattered, scattered but his words soothe my wounds.

I remember that morning when my dad passed away. The world lost its color, the sun's rays refracted with an ominous glow, and the air felt heavy and dense. I remember I did not sob my heart out; I did not cry; I did not tear off my clothes and start moaning in sadness. I remember there was no explosive rage, no slamming doors, no breaking glasses, or smashing things. I remember I quietly went to a room, my eyes started gazing at a wooden chair in silence, sometimes at the ceiling of the room. And my heart was pounding, I guess angels were not there on that day to breathe with me. I was slowly devoured by memories and then fell asleep. When the night slipped into the day, I suddenly burst into tears, like I had heard the news that day. It was on that day that I stopped reading signs, I discredited time and the universe, I adopted silence for my soul and imprisoned all my affectionate aspects, that day I died, and no one saw it. That day I was born, and nobody noticed.

I know many men want sons, but not many sons will have a father like him. All I wish for is that one day I can become a father as good as he was to me.

***

Beloved Olena Petrovych,

My dear Olena, loneliness is like the presence of a creature with awe and terror. Like a snake that coils around your entire body and slowly advances to crush your bones, a black sticky substance that starts from the walls of the room and gradually spreads throughout the house. Like a painful thought that slowly takes over your entire soul and mind, like a small and insidious creature. At these times, even in the busiest crowds, there is loneliness. I feel hopeless about the things and people that are absent, and how much their presence would be helpful in these moments, and how loneliness dares to come so close in their absence. On those days, I do not feel like uttering any words, instead, I announce a day of silence. On those days I tend to take a walk, climb a hill, sit somewhere high, watch the sun disappear peacefully behind the clouds covering the sky. Or I tend to walk across a shoreline and then sit by the ocean, enjoying the sun to walk out the sky at the end of the other side of the ocean, gorgeously, yet silently.

In the depths of my soul, I have cried out for the soothing balm of silence for what seems like an eternity. But when the long-awaited stillness finally enveloped me, I was consumed with an overwhelming sense of dread, searching for any sound to fill the void and keep me from the dark abyss of my thoughts. How disappointing it was, this paradox of mine. I had grown too accustomed to the constant noise of the world around me - the voices of people, traffic noise, TV, radio, birdsong, and even the shrill cries of my neighbors. It all grated on my nerves, except for the sweet song of birds, whose melodies I longed to hear in isolation. I dreamt of being in a place where there is not a single extraneous sound. But even at the dacha, I stopped hearing the silence. It was as though the absence of sound only amplified my own thoughts; the cacophony of my mind overwhelmed me. I wanted to scream, just to drown out everything around me. And yet, when I finally found myself in a place where the only sound was the beating of my own heart, I was struck with a profound sense of terror. The stillness was deafening, suffocating, threatening to consume me whole. Even the gentle rustle of the wind had vanished, leaving me adrift in a sea of silence.

Last night, the room was too quiet. The television remained silent in the next room, the neighbors were fast asleep, and not a soul stirred on the street outside - not even a whisper of the wind could be heard. I know it should have been the time for rejoicing, but I was caught in the grip of panic instead. I fell asleep on the phone. When I woke up, I noticed that I spent the entire night waiting for you in silence, hoping to hear your voice on the other end. Reluctantly I warned my memory to remember why pain abounded. Why were my legs heavy? Why were my hands shaking? I woke up sweating in a cruel loneliness that caressed my arms and wrapped my soul with such insistence that I had no choice but to hold it to my chest and hug it with resignation. A single ray of light appeared that illuminated my drowsy body, dawn struck me in the face and remorse awaited me already tired at the foot of the bed, he looked at me with courage. —You called her all night and she never answered!

Last night, I called. All I wanted from you was to come out of your room and look up to the sky; the moon waited patiently for you to notice her. I wanted to ask you to walk out of your room and behold its aesthetic beauty, its captivating allure. Embrace its glimpse into the wonders of the universe. I remember you told me that, on the darkest nights, she had offered you everything, that its gentle and serene glow has captivated your hearts for years. Naked and bright, despite spending most of her nights hiding her wrinkled ridges in the shadows, yet only offered you shining pieces of herself in case you needed a little lighter.

I accepted that dawn by force and took refuge in my uncontrollable crying in the softness of my body under the covers. I was not ready to calm down, I was not ready to get back up.

***

Dearest Brother,

It was just the other night when our mother asked about the nighttime wonder that envelopes the streets of Wroclaw. She knows well my fervor for the nights - the glowing moon, the starry skies - and I indulged her with tales that I shall now inscribe in this letter for you.

The nighttime here is a never-ending mystery that keeps feeding the souls of strangers. You should come soon and experience it with me and Olena. A stroll through the streets of Wroclaw on a starlit night is an enchanting experience. The soft light illuminates the cobblestone streets, creating a tranquil atmosphere that is both peaceful and inspiring. The night sky is a beautiful and mysterious canvas that has captivated humans for centuries. It is a wonder that inspires poets, artists, and dreamers alike, whether standing under a canopy of stars in a remote location or simply gazing out of a bedroom window. November 18th, the lights of garlands are already flickering in the windows, Wroclaw's decorations are appearing in city cafes and on the streets, and the Christmas Tree is opened in the Center of Wroclaw Market Square. This morning I woke up and saw snow flickering outside the window. After the rampage of October colors, on the eve of a snowy winter, nature seems to calm down. Lately, I often hear the phrase that November is considered the darkest month of the year. But this is true!

The monotonous colors of the earth and trees, morning mists, thorny rains, and fierce winds undoubtedly create a rather mystical atmosphere for nature. When did winter come? Where has autumn gone so quickly? As I approach my third month here, I have come to realize that, as the stars twinkle in the sky above, the people of Wroclaw emerge to enjoy the night. The restaurants and bars are filled with laughter and chatter, and the sounds of music and dancing fill the air. The vibrant cityscape is transformed by the shimmering stars, and the air is filled with the gentle hum of nightlife. The stars keep emerging, one by one until the sky is illuminated with a blanket of glittering light. The moon, a glowing orb in the distance, illuminates the world below, casting its gentle light upon the city. The constellations, like old friends, take their place in the sky, telling the stories of ancient mythologies and providing a sense of order in the midst of chaos. I am afraid I often find myself out of words! Staring at the moon and beholding her beauty, her phases of waxing and waning are spellbinding. From a sliver of silver to a full orb of glowing light, the moon's presence adds an element of mystery and romance to the night sky.

For me, the night sky is not just about beauty and wonder though. It is also a reminder of my place in the universe, and of the vastness of the world around me. Looking up at the stars, it is hard not to feel small and insignificant but also inspired and in awe. The night sky is a reminder to look beyond the world I know and to imagine the infinite possibilities that lie beyond. It invites me to dream, to wonder, to contemplate the mysteries of life. So please brother, next time you find yourself under a starry sky, take a moment to appreciate its mystery and vastness, and let your imagination soar and walk you to introspection. And come to Wroclaw please, let us walk in its streets at night and you shall understand the words I wrote. I will wait for you to come.

***

One day, as you sit and pour your tea into the cup, your mind wanders through thousands of layers of thoughts, and reaches that dark point that you have never been able to see, always remaining a mystery to you. And when you are finally able to catch a glimpse of it, you can hardly believe that it is here, in this cup, on this carpet, with these people, but with a different mood that suddenly blurs everything into ambiguity for a brief moment.

We all have had moments where we thought we had lived this life before and seen and said what we are seeing and saying, and there are many theories about it, and people constantly speculate about it. I always experience these moments when the light is shining, the air is fresh, and my mother's voice comes to me, telling me about her life with a special sadness. Perhaps science, mysticism, philosophy, and religions may offer different explanations for it, but at least I understand that even if my body and soul have evolved from thousands of years ago and I carry memories and patterns of my ancestors, or if I live in another world, two things that have always been the most vivid in my life are the light and my mother.

***

To you my love,

I am afraid my eyes will shine when I am talking about you, or I will start to grin when someone compliments you. Or my hands will tremble, my body will shiver when your delicate voice flows into my ears. I am afraid that people might spell me out in my details without knowing it as I cannot hide my love for you anymore. It is all over my face.

"Why do you write of her so often?"

they often ask, knowing full well the answer. It seems they have noticed I write about you abundantly.

I think about us often, and that makes me float on the clouds and write poems about the wind waiting for you in this living dream, which only exists because of you. Speak to me of your favorite words, and I shall mold them into beautiful and profound sighs that will adorn your dreams, serving as a pillow. Let me show you how this feather dances with delight for you, conjuring dancing letters that just want to exist around your precious name. Take me in, the only familiar border, for when you are around, it fills my heart with a warm feeling, and by then, I am willing to live in an old cottage with a large kitchen and a small cafe. Where I am sitting on windowsills curled up with a book, looking at the big garden as the rays seep between the maze of branches. And there you are, enjoying the sunshine in the big garden, breathing fresh air while the fresh air alerts your senses. You start singing to our plant babies and growing roses in the garden. Or maybe to live in a small apartment in Barcelona or Paris city, filled with lights and plants and the smell of freshly baked bread. A place where you are standing on a cliff overlooking the ocean and your white cat trailing behind you. And when I have become a bookworm, collecting my own library, working on my writings, and feeling alive, chanting all day to myself "Nothing matters anymore".

My love, I assure you I still fail to know if you are the glow from early morning or the light reflecting from the ocean, for I find your heart to be alluring and the world seems to slow all the way down when I am with you. Sometimes when you rattle my heart, all that I can do is sit and feel the breeze of the cosmos whispering into my veins, and who knows!? Maybe this is what they say when they tell you to be alive. You are like a flame inside me that warms me and that is what I love about my life lately. Especially when I am walking into the winter night and the wave of cold is taking over all my skin. I want you to know every time I see you, it is like a fresh brush stroke across my canvass, bright and wet. For you move my soul like tides of the sea. You make me so ready to burst into a thousand wild flames. You move a mountain of joy inside my chest. I know I did not want "someone" like you, but rather I wanted you specifically. That is the difference between those who are looking for something, and me, who inadvertently ended up finding everything.

Oh, if only I could be one of the teardrops of yours. Gently, I would fall from the crystal-clear wells of your eyes, slowly tracing the curve of your cheek, and finally, I would descend upon your trembling lips. Oh, if only for a brief moment, I could wander within the pupil of your eyes, revolving around its circumference. If only I could be that teardrop of yours, which dries before it falls, leaving its mark on your dewy lashes for minutes to come. You were so... so lovable. I hope that you remember me in the middle of the night. That when you laugh out loud, you want me to be there laughing with you. And if loving you means I must become an enemy to myself, then so be it. I am going in. I'll go into the war against myself, and I will win battles, one by one, for you.

***

Wroclaw, February 9, 2020

I like to look endlessly at how peacefully and quietly white fluffy clouds float in my window room. They fascinate me with their bizarre shapes, their deceptive texture, and their proximity, gradually relaxing and unraveling the tangles of restless thoughts that hang like a lead weight on tired shoulders. I used to look at the stars for a long time. I peered into this endless space, trying to find answers. But looking at the clouds I am not looking for answers, because here they are, on the surface, I do not need to look for them.

I cherish the days when a clear sky with a slowly floating cotton wool of clouds suddenly begins to darken rapidly, and then a downpour falls on you with noise. The wind rises, swift and gusty, tearing the delicate cherry petals from the branches, lifting them into the air and whirling until they soar to the sky, and you rush home, holding a wide straw hat with one hand, the hem of a loose summer dress with the other. And in the distance, the heavy chime of the bells of a rural church is already ringing. Or on cold days, when the dank fingers of fog rummage around the ground in search of a lair and an incomparable feeling of wholeness and comfort awakens inside me. Hiding from the sharp slaps of the wind, I am happy to visit my favorite paintings in galleries and museums. I enjoy my semi-fairy-like existence. I want to always be surrounded by beauty and things that bring aesthetic pleasure,

I dream of making my life similar to a fairy tale, liken to its work of art, enjoying every impulse, bowed, like a violin trill. Be fully myself. Lately, I go for a walk alone in the park nearby. There is this place - benches around a strange installation in the shape of hands. But it is my favorite spot. It is where I feel... in the world. Even though the cold has already arrived, I still want to go back there - to that iron bench. To grab some tea and just watch the local residents ride by on their bicycles. And think about something grand. I am a contemplator by nature. All my life I have been following the continuous movement of the world, a free dance of the winds, tiny points of aircraft above my head, gestures of hands, and the wandering views of people sitting opposite. I saw a unit changed to a deuce, invisible to break in half for two millennia, and now I calmly observe how the years slip away with their chaotic course.

I am not afraid that life will leak, melting like the first November snow. I am just afraid that she will carry her beauty past me, not allowing me to behold them more attentively. I fear to die before I get the chance to read those good books I planned to read, to inhale the scent of novels with a cup of coffee in my hand, the soulful songs, and mesmerizing voices I wanted to listen to, the terrific stories I was keen to hear, the movies I loved to watch. I love walking along the edge of a mountain and jumping from great heights. I want to travel the world on foot, no matter the season, because nature is my calling. I could spend years in the forest and never tire of it, as long as I survive. It is not that I do not value my life or that I am brave. In fact, I am quite afraid. I am afraid that all these beauties that life offers me, and I go to my grave not discovering them.

***

Wroclaw, February 12, 2020

As I stand by the Odra River, gazing into its murky depths and watching the waves crash against the shore. The river, with its endless flow, seems to mock my ephemeral existence, reminding me of the relentless passage of time. I can feel the weight of my decisions pressing down on me. It is a dreadful thing to be young and plagued by the constant fear that time is slipping away and you have yet to make your mark on the world. So, I plead to the river one more time: Devour me, make me your eternal embryo! Closing my eyes, I want to dream, but I see only pitch darkness. In trying to look into this darkness, I hope to see at least a small ray of light in it. A ray of light that will illuminate my dark path, but every time I try, I see only pitch darkness.

Yet, I keep trying to pick myself up by whispering to my heart that I have to learn to turn the page without fear of finding myself empty and assuming that another chapter in my life has ended. Another one begins soon, the novel is still ongoing, and I have more stories to live and new characters to meet. I must read calmly. I will soon be in my best scene. But then the insidious voice of doubt creeps in, whispering,

"What if this is the final page of your story?",

The bubbles of hope burst, and I am left feeling small and vulnerable once again.

While standing aside and watching how other people live, as a butterfly frozen in amber, I exist. While people are fumbling through bags at an incredible speed in search of an umbrella to protect themselves from rain and snow, I gladly expose my face to cold drops. The ink was probably smeared on the cheeks, red from the cold, and the hands were so cold that it was hard to type. But for the first time in what feels like ages, I finally feel... Normal!

But what if I were to disappear? For a moment. For a second. For eternity! Hide from everything, avoid confrontation. Sail away forever in an unknown direction. Surround myself with clouds or desperately warm myself with golden flames. Or perhaps pause for a moment to cleanse my soul? But what if it is all an illusion? For I feel I am different from what I was yesterday. I am a white flag. Conscious of events, unaware of the future. Uncertain in the certainty of destiny. I desire something beyond the mere trappings of humanity. I want to be a tragedy written by Shakespeare. A sword used to kill a valiant knight. A flame that burns a love letter. An ocean in which sailors drown. The old monastery, in which the monks die of old age. A piano played by a sad poet. I do not know what to say or how but sometimes I want to solve all the problems at once. To save this world. But I know it is impossible. There are things we cannot change. Many times, I have thought about writing this text, but every time, as I sat down, the words, like a flock of pigeons, flew off to the corners, and I could not catch them. But today, with frozen hands and uneven breaths on this winter day, I managed to catch a few. I keep reiterating to my poor self to lean in. The good, the bad, the ugly…lean in. To tuck away soaring and happy moments because I know I will need them when that house of cards comes crashing down. I try to go about my day just like the prey bird goes about its day, finding food, nesting, and doing whatever they do, knowing that at any moment the hawk can swoop in and end it all.

***

Time is playing games with me!

There's a large wooden clock hanging on the wall, mocking me and saying, "You're doing exactly what you wanted with your life, but why aren't you happy?" From the corner of its eye, it gazes at me, and with a tone that makes me feel ridiculed, it says, "Come and catch it." It throws some of my big desires right in front of my face and continues, "Come on! The ones you wanted. Gather them and smile." It tilts its head and points to its lips.

I try to ponder its words, make an effort to understand and listen, but it seems like one of my ears is ajar, and the other is a gate. A gate that a stone ball has shattered its lock, and the gatekeeper no longer cares about excessive thinking! With fear and stress, I tell myself to gather my wishes quickly, so that "time" will not regret, but as I come to myself, I realize it hasn't looked at me and has been behind my back! I rush into the history class at seven o'clock on Saturday, and this time, contrary to the entire year, I take a deep breath.

We have suffered so much these days that when we see our dreams within arm's reach, we get scared, forget that they were our desires, and push them away!

***

The church stands like a sentinel, its spire reaching toward the night sky, beckoning the moon to come closer. Another lonely night with only my thoughts for company. The street is quiet, except for the occasional barking of dogs, the wind howls like a mournful song through the empty streets, and the glow of the orange streetlights reflects in the windows like distant stars. Life is a swift moment that rushes by like a comet through the velvety blackness of the sky. I am therefore pushed to make every effort to fluff up the tail of this comet with the sparkling fire of my flaming heart. I put my hand on the glass and leave an imprint that is barely visible. The night is here to stay. It wraps me in its cold embrace, and I huddle beneath a blanket that offers no warmth. It chills me to the bone. I recall the words of a man I once encountered on a subway when I asked him if it is possible to love and avoid it at the same time, and he said "Certainly, yes.", he paused for a moment and then said "I simply protect myself, and it has worked since I started applying it. I give affection sincerely and limitlessly, yet I can distance myself, if necessary, without remorse. I depart with peace of mind because, unlike those who have crossed my path, I strive to leave footprints and never scars."

I remember the words of my mother, who once said "If you like someone, son, do not go so fast, proceed gradually, without haste, for there is time for everything. Do not fall in love like now, do it the old way, with chocolates and flowers, with trips to the park, with unexpected surprises, without lavish gifts. Do not be jealous, but rather, understanding. Do not be angry; rather, empathize with her, for we all have problems. And I assure you, she will not be an exception. Do not treat her unkindly, nor toy with her. Be a gentleman, treat her like a lady. Shield her when she needs it, make her feel safe when she feels insecure. When she is in her days, hug her and fill her with pampering, if she wants to cry, give her reasons to smile. But above everything, if you truly love her, make her feel so yours, and that you are hers, so that despite all the adversities that come your ways, nothing separates you two."

I recall the words you once wrote to me, too. "You love to be alone, like that little gust of wind that always rushes alone, but to you, just like someone is hooked to the wind, a leaflet that was accidentally captured will fly with you, but this will not last long and will soon fly away on its own."

Time flies too fast and sometimes I do not even notice how it slips away like a ghost of days gone by. It is a bitter irony to look back now and remember those good times and heartfelt conversations. You remember wanting to squeeze every last drop out of those moments, to savor them forever. But now you see that you are holding sand in your hands and the grains are escaping through your fingers.

My love, bear with me please, for I know all too well how arduous it can be to love me. To know me is a sad odyssey without a destination, but as soon as I gain confidence, I will be there in every trouble that you do not know how to hide. When I tell you that you are important to me, it means that whenever I see you, I am the happiest. Whenever I am by your side, I am filled with energy. When I hear your voice, I am at peace.

When you are not around, I miss you the most. When I say I love you, it does not matter how many hours we have spent together and how close I have been to you. As soon as we separated, I long for you, and this longing continues until I see you again. When I say you are my priority, it means that it does not matter if I am watching my favorite movie, doing my favorite work, being in a busy and exciting crowd, or even breaking apart and crying from intense sorrow. In the most bored and impatient state, the world loses its luster in the wake of your message, and in those precious seconds, I cast aside all else to indulge in our conversation. You have become a constant part of me. I constantly crave you, your memories, your presence, your love, your words, your laughter, and everything about you. I wonder if you understand this state? Darling, since I have known you, the songs have made sense like never before. I want you to know that even after many weeks, I still go out at night to that same street of Wroclaw where we bid our last farewell, and the soft cold breeze whispers the last words you said to me. I close my eyes and I can imagine your image, down to the smallest detail. I continue to feel tired; I continue to drive over trifles. I do not like uncertainty so much, it is unbearable, but now my life is mired in them. I want everything to be good at the snap of my fingers, but it does not happen. It does not happen, never has been, and never will be. It is not a pulp novel; it is not a Disney movie – it is just my life.

For many years, I locked myself away from the outside world in my dim-lit room, where only the characters created by my imagination kept me company. For years, I eavesdropped on the conversations of these nonexistent people with impunity.

I shamelessly peered into their souls, into their bedrooms and water closets. I followed every movement of their pens as they wrote love letters and wills. I watched devotees praying to their gods, murderers in the act of killing, and children in their secret games. The doors of prisons and brothels were flung open before me; sailing ships and camel caravans transported me across seas and deserts; centuries and continents changed at my whim. I saw the spiritual insignificance of the greats of this world and the nobility of the orphans and the poor. I bent so low over the beds of the sleepers that they could feel my breath on their faces. I saw their dreams. My room was filled with characters waiting for me to write about them, but lately, I keep choosing you.

***

To Olena,

If you are well, that is good, but as for me, I cannot say the same. I sit here writing for you with a heavy heart, a heart weighed down by the burden of sorrow that I cannot seem to shake. The days seem long and never-ending, each one dragging on in a monotonous cycle that feels devoid of any joy or happiness. I try to pick up the pieces and move on, but the weight of my sorrow drags me down like an anchor. The sun rises, but its light seems dim and muted, unable to dispel the darkness that has taken root in my soul.

Every morning, I wake up to the same reality: The parallel universes that appear in my dreams, closely mirroring my everyday life yet twisted into a nightmarish state, bring me no joy. After such dreams, I often get up in the morning broken and confused, because my soul is still trembling from night experiences and events. Then for another half an hour, I walk around the apartment, confused, trying to shake off the scraps of another reality. My world is devoid of the things that once pleased me, the things that gave my life meaning and purpose. The sounds of laughter and music that once filled my ears are now replaced by an eerie silence, one that echoes loudly through the emptiness of my life. It is as if the world around me has stopped turning, and I am left standing amid a desolate wasteland.

Sometimes, when the night is especially dark and lonely, I find myself thinking of you, and the memories of the good times we shared. My anguishes and I often lie on the arms of those nights where our only star is your smile. But even those memories of us and those smiles of yours bring a little comfort, for they serve only to remind me of what I miss. Because for a moment I was getting better. For a moment I felt good. For a moment I wanted to live. For a moment I had hope again. And in an instant, I lost everything again. My darling, I truly believe that sometimes we do not realize how badly we have been treated until someone comes into our life who treats us right, and we do not know how to react to so much affection.

Now that your absence stares at my soul, I wonder if you are going to smile when you hear my name, or you are going to groan as if I have stolen something precious from you? I wonder if your heart can still feel me. It is that the world can whip us, try to widen distances, occupy our time, and make the effort to break us but as long as we know there is an eternal truth to which we can return all the time, there is a force that resides in the heart. The certainty of being loved unconditionally and knowing that if we are sad, tired, exhausted, or jaded by this world, we can find rest, warmth, understanding, and love in the arms of another, is the greatest gift that life has given us. So, hold me tight in your thoughts and make of these eternal moments, a single being, a single love, a single beat in time, just you and me. My dear Olena, my mind is confused and full of unanswered questions. I do not know what to write to you, but you know how tragic this situation is for me. Small longings resound as echoes in my body, causing my muscles to tremble. I no longer wait for much because waiting serves no purpose. It brings a wave of sadness, covered with the foam of excitement. But when this foam dissipates, nostalgia flows out. But then I question myself, my theory, that perhaps waiting does have its own purpose, that it may serve a purpose. Maybe waiting is what gives everything meaning. Waiting for something, someone, for dreams to come true. But what if we stop waiting for anything? Was what we wanted what we needed? Did chasing after it have a purpose? And what if we wait for someone for too long? For an image or for someone we truly know. What do we really need?

I need to ask a favor from you now if I may. If you saw the moon tonight, ask her about me. The way I keep asking her about you every night. Ask her why I never stop writing about love. Ask her why this love will live only by waiting. Ask her if she would like to fill us again with her light soon. Ask her if she misses seeing us both under her light, the way I miss seeing both of us, holding cups of hot coffee. And laughing, heading back to the dormitory in those cold nights of Wroclaw. Ask her if she yearns for our heartfelt conversations that floated away into the abyss of time, drifting on waves of love, led by the sails of paper secrets and the compass of ink.

I am afraid. I am afraid of the knots that will not loosen in your chest. Avoid the mirrors, avoid the reflections. We must forever close our eyes to the prolific verb of forgetfulness. So here I am, with nothing but the pain of my sorrow for company. I can only hope that this letter finds you in better spirits and that you are not weighed down by the same sadness that consumes me.

***

It has been about six days since I last wrote. I believe it started precisely when I told myself that by the end of this past week, I would tidy up my scattered play and keep it stored on my phone, ready for the moment I have been waiting for so long. Since then, my pen has not written anything, and my mind, filled with thoughts that had piled up and had nowhere to release, decayed. A deep pit was formed, and the stench of rotten words twisted within my brain.

The more it grew, the more my state deteriorated until yesterday when it reached perfect harmony, and with an unknown force, I managed to write five lines forcefully, with one particular word repeating about ten times within that piece. "Affection," "affection," "affection," "affection," "affection," and "affection." It was as if all the words accumulated in my mind were yearning for autumn and merely cried out for a specific month together. They had chosen the topic and the text themselves and chanted their name ten times within those five lines, yet if I were to say, I loved just one sentence and one line of it, and no one, not even myself, could read the rest of the writing correctly, not even following the punctuation marks!

In short, I could not write, and all the words attacked my soul, leaving a mark on my body. Since I am not my true self without writing, I am forced to pretend, and I can say that in conversations with everyone, I am pretending to be myself.

***

My dearest Olena Petrovych,

I know I met you in October, yet it feels as if we had known each other before then. Perhaps, you were the vast, unfathomable sea, and I was merely a wave, ever drawn to your magnetic pull. That night, when we first spoke, I remember gazing upon you as one does in the tales of love, you looked back in a way that made me want to ditch everything and bring your heart all the love of the universe. It was only a gaze that lasted for two seconds, but why did it feel like my heart had bloomed for two hundred years?

Have I mentioned to you that I went to Cinema City Wroclavia to watch "1917" upon your recommendation of the movie? The experience was a surreal one, with the movie's gripping storyline, the ambiance of the cinema, the hum of voices, the bustling city, and the frigid, overcast night all felt so vividly real. Yet, amidst all of this, there was a poignant absence, the absence of the dream I held of spending that night with you.

To tell you the truth, the past few days have been very difficult for me, I feel like a lump is in my throat and I have difficulty keeping a grip on the flow of my thoughts. I am struggling a lot with what happened after that night. I am not sure how I must feel about it, should I be in shock? Shall I be in disbelief? At times, it feels like a nightmare I cannot escape. I try to flee from it all. I close my eyes wanting the whole thing to evaporate soon, hoping all of these could fade away. I walk by the Odra River to forget everything about that night and us. Yet, you linger in my mind, even as I try to push you away. It is hard as I see you every week in university classes.

It seems the further I run away from you, the faster I come back to you. And the more I ponder our situation, the greater my anguish. And for that, I am tremendously tired and exhausted. For seven long days, I have confined myself to this room. I am tired of everything, tired of myself, my room, my books, my handwritten notes, and this damn window that reminds me of your world every moment. I lie down in bed for hours and do nothing, yet I would still feel tired. I am tired of waiting, tired of getting no calls, waiting on messages, and hoping for your name to pop on my screen. How much longer must I wait until your late-night message arrives? Your letter is late, too! Maybe it is because you do not know what to write. But let me assure you that all you have to do is to write your name! because I promise it will heal my wounded heart. I am not particularly concerned with what you write to me but that you write to me, that you have not forgotten me.

For I still search for you on the road, in the city, when I pass the spots, we have been to. I am fatigued by the absence of you, that crazy absence that hits me stronger in my solitude. You are like a shadow in my life, following, watching, biting. I am also tired of living in the good old past, tired of creating "our" life, and how things will work out in the end. The apathy seems to have completely taken over me. One of the most melancholic situations, in my opinion, is when two people genuinely connect on a deep level and share intimate details about themselves: their dreams, their future, their fears, their "what ifs", their favorite things, what they cherish, what they despise, truly everything, and they go back to being outsiders, pretending to be strangers. It is like two strangers who run into each other in a dark alley and then never remember each other again, you have to walk past them and pretend like you never knew them, never even talked to them before.

Wild times. I exist. And I can tell you it is the worst feeling ever. Not good, not bad. Just here. A dispersed, ethereal being, among the darkness of thought, sailing without finding myself in any port and seeing the ocean of the world from spatial distances. I lose myself in abstractions, in silence, in solitude.

There is a final goodbye that is coming, and I sense it in the very air. I am forced to take a step. I am ready.

***

I remain in a state where dawn breaks, and on more than one occasion, I wake up unaware of what surprise awaits once the sun rises. Insistent tears filled with pain, an air of despair or immeasurable anger. Yet, it is not so much about what precedes, but rather when the sky darkens. Each night, I live in uncertainty, moving between the sheets in a back-and-forth motion, searching for the sleep that has long denied me rest, yearning for the pain to end, hoping for something better. In my dreams, I live what I have lost in reality. My friends, my mom, my sunshine. The life I cannot go back to. Walks at sunset, conversations in a cafe, buying sweets, a smile that I can never find. It seems that I need to move on, that it would be right, but in reality, I do not know what to look for and how to find something new when everything I need is left behind. I have mastered pretending by now, denying myself and my feelings. My condition is deteriorating. Recently a tsunami came. A wave that was supposed to sweep me away once and for all. An event that robbed me of any sense. My mind is finally refusing to obey. It no longer has the strength to reproduce previously acquired information, and memory and concentration are so distant to me. For two months now, I only got out of bed to go where I have to be. I do not want anyone to suspect anything. I come back and cover myself with a blanket. I cannot even sleep anymore. I feel like tons of plastic drifting in isolation on the surface of the ocean, not even worthy of recycling.

I began the year with fear, facing that unknown world called university life. Many see it as a new experience in their lives, but in my case, it was different, an unfamiliar place with unfamiliar people, unsure if I would be able to adapt and fit in among the others. Months passed, and nothing seemed to improve. Everything became more difficult. Trying to fit in, being more outgoing—what once made me stand out among others had completely vanished here. Once, I asked the sky to pour with rain because I hoped that seeing the sky cry, the world would mourn with me. But the world paid no attention. It continued to live, time continued to move on, seasons changed one after the other, and plants around me were born and died. The world did not wait. The world never waits. The fear of rejection made me more distant, more withdrawn, and sadder, and I felt surrounded by people yet utterly alone. Since I did not know what to feel, I acted like I did not feel anything. Until she arrived, I did not expect her to come and change a part of me in such a sweet way, but at the same time leaving me in complete agony, as she became a double-edged sword.

***

I am underwater. At the bottom of an ocean.

I swim and with the movements of my hands and feet, I push away the stones that surround me. Stones that have become the thoughts of my days. I move forward and search for ideas that have caused me to dive into the ocean. The further I go, the more the stones accumulate, and I find myself farther from the place I belong, with no way back. I do not know how deep I am in the water, but it feels like the end. I cannot go any deeper from here.

Once again, I try to remind myself why I came here. I do not know if you have ever experienced this feeling before, the sensation of being trapped in the depths of the water, searching for something specific. The depth increases, and the path back becomes harder. It is as if the water carries you away to a place where you become more confused, instead of reaching what you desire.

I am confused now. A confused person who is more longing for the shore than ever before.

***

To Olena Petrovych,

In philosophy books, they do not teach us that life is more sincere in the airport and bus terminals. It is in these places where kisses between lovers and tears of "see you soon or forever" reveal every raw emotion, leaving nothing hidden. Everything hurts more when you feel that little fire in your chest that there is no genuine place in the world: If you leave, a small piece of mine remains with you, and if you return, you bring back what was missing.

The words "Please stay a little longer" and "But what if another bus comes soon" are some of the most honest declarations of love one can ever make. Walking slowly to have you a little bit again or perhaps choosing to continue down the hall without looking back, hoping it will hurt less that way, the feeling that maybe I did not say everything that needed to be said, or that I had talked too much, the kisses on the forehead, the hugs that are balm and bland, shaking hands, and the farewell in the air are all sincere love declarations in the airport and bus terminals.

I am at Wrocław Bus Station, and I must write this, I must bid farewell to you and the tranquility you once offered, for it has been replaced by a turbulent storm, making it impossible for me to stay. And the time of farewell is here. A time when time itself ceases to flow, but silent streams of tears flow instead. Their current carves valleys on pale, tired cheeks. The air is filled with sorrow, despair, and suffering. The scream that cannot escape tears through the cells of the body, one by one. The pain in my chest quickly reaches every muscle and rips through my body as if it weighs nothing. Like a feather tossed by the force of the wind, like a glider descending into a downward current. And I finally realize that I can no longer do anything, that I have lost control. People around me want to help me carry this burden, but I already sense, I already know, that it is the end. The verdict was made long ago. It was just a matter of time. It is over, what never even became a story, not even the slightest paragraph can be told. It was like a subtle sentence. You were just a tender glance from afar, with a provocative silhouette that only came to take away the cherry blossoms, like an unexpected April gust of wind… I am writing you my last words, although it never crossed my mind that one day I would sit and write them. I always imagined spending eternity crafting beautiful poetry to apply a smile to your lips, but life has its own twists and turns that leave us reeling.

I never intended to coerce you into loving me; rather, I wish you were aware of how much I fought for you. There were moments when I would shut down to repair your light, depleting my own energy and remaining in the shadows just to witness your radiance. While it is true that you did not solicit my affections, it is also true that love does not require permission. Perhaps you cared, but not enough to spare me the heartache of bidding farewell. Now, I venture out only in darkness, as the light reminds me of the one, I bestowed upon you. A light I will never retrieve. I admit I could not distinguish where you ended and where my motherland began, and for that, I tried hard to cling to the rope of hope with my back teeth and fought life with honor to build something for us. But even the honorable ones lose their battles, even the good people collapse under the weight of a burden they simply could not hold anymore. And now I leave the battlefield like a defeated knight with my bleeding hands and scars all over my heart. I leave because I have nothing more to fight for.

***

Nuremberg, May 3, 2020

I love to bring a little drama into my everyday life, for without it, life would be insipid and dull. Today I was sitting in a dimly lit living room, listening to a selection of music on YouTube called "Playlist for Depressed Poets" and drinking hot tea. I looked at the setting sun, then at the burgundy curtains, compelling me to imagine that I dwelled within an ancient abode. When the violin began to sound, I felt a sudden sense of displacement, as if I were no longer at home in the world I had always known. A sense of otherworldliness overtook me as if I were transported to a realm beyond my own. It was a pleasant feeling. One cannot help but wonder why the people of bygone centuries were so uniquely captivating, with their eloquent speech and grandiose lifestyles. I like to believe it was the enchanting melodies of classical music that had the power to ignite the imagination, to imbue every word with an otherworldly charm. Go turn on some masterworks by Johann Sebastian Bach or Chopin and tell me you suddenly do not feel like composing a handwritten love letter to your beloved "Annabelle", infused with the melancholy that imbues the finest of poetry.

Imagine, if you will, living in the 19th century, being the student of an old scientist or writer who perceives your aptitude for knowledge. In return, you clean his house, cook and take care of them. From morning to afternoon, he teaches you to write, read literature, and then proceed to geometry. In the evening you go for a walk through the lush gardens, conversing about historical events and the nuances of art. At the same time, you communicate in another language to train speech and grammar. You wear beautiful light dresses, and comfortable shoes with small heels, and you always gather your hair up, coming up with different hairstyles.

Sometimes I just want a doctor from the nineteenth century to come into the house, shake his head over me, and strictly forbid everyone in the family to disturb me. Frightened by my nervous exhaustion, he would prescribe rest, peace, and fulfillment of all my whims as a treatment. I, in turn, pledge to dutifully fulfill my part of the deal, namely: to gaze out of the window with a mournful expression, to appear paler than usual, to have intermittent fits of hysteria, to display a lack of interest in people and walks, and to yearn for something unattainable, something that no one could procure for me. Just leave me alone in some abandoned family estate of a long-disappeared aristocratic family, surrounded by an icy lake and a foggy forest, and I will happily live my days in his walls damp from long desolation, reading swollen books from a huge family library by candlelight and studying the cracked portraits in desert rooms.

Or in my other fantasies, I study the ancient Greek epic in the huge dark library of an old castle surrounded by fog. Sleep creeps up to the heavy oak doors, tickles the windows with bony knotted fingers, and sings terrible lullabies. But I have no time to sleep. I relate to the legends of monsters, bloody battles, and terrible birth curses. I imagine myself in the role of an angry god, a brave hero, or a bloodthirsty monster guarding a narrow strait.

I try on a thousand faces and live a thousand lives. If I had immortality, I would spend it studying literature, philosophy, and arts. The whole eternity would open in front of me, exposing its secrets. The fabric of the universe would unravel from books, the fortress walls of decaying castles, and dusty archival scrolls, and I would unravel them all, frantically seeking to uncover the truth. Why? To confirm that beyond the final veil lurks a limitless array of hiding places, because this world will never reveal all of its secrets.

***

Nuremberg, September 5, 2020

Autumn has arrived once again, and with it comes my familiar routine of long Saturday walks through the park. For some reason, I have been waiting for this autumn dullness. Along with a cold mist, peace descended on my soul, I seem to be in my element: I no longer need to squeeze out a smile on my face in order to please the sun that has lingered in my area. Yet, in recent years of my life, autumn reminds me of getting old and gray hair, as if the leaves falling from the trees symbolize the inevitable decay of my body.

Though I am somewhere in the middle of being young and old, the thought of aging is a haunting one. The gradual loss of grace, the crumpling of once firm and youthful faces, the silvering of hair, the trembling hands, and the weakening legs that struggle to keep up with a walk. Perhaps this is why people usually die at ages less than eighty years old. For if one were to live two hundred years, he would have been ravaged by excessive longing for things that were no longer possible to have.

Can I just be at age 40 and have my peace then? I silently plead sometimes. For I fear a slow death, a death where I am a senile old man on a hospital bed, where doctors come and make health reports about my health conditions to later read them to whoever is watching me. Concise reports, nearly the same from one day to the next. Not even slight changes in my health. Just a pitiful old man, asleep on a hospital bed, whose life is fading away, his death is approaching, slowly but certainly! "Let me lie there then, in a deep sleep for a while.", I cry out. So that one day, maybe sooner than they predict, I will quietly sleep forever. It is for this reason that I want to take a thousand beautiful photos, not to post them on some social media but to look back upon them with fondness in my old age, remembering with a smile how young and beautiful myself and my friends were. Because sometimes it seems as if the magic of a certain moment exists only in the time of that moment. That it often feels as though the magic of a moment is confined to the fleeting instant in which it occurs. You know these moments should be protected and guarded like a snowflake that may rest in your palm for a while and then suddenly melts, becomes a drop, and flows away. And no matter how much we may try to recreate moments like these, with the same people and in the same places, they will never be the same.

Walking down the train of thought in my head, I see my younger self going out into nature, with or without a book, leafing through the book, allowing nature to touch my soul and heart in areas that no other could do in search of a "face". As a child, I used to believe I was destined to undertake a noble quest that would change the world irrevocably, for the better. Yet, as I grow older, I am starting to believe this is not the case. I see myself simply as a part of the whole, a link in time, a letter in a word, and hopefully taking the good things from the past and delivering them into a future beyond myself. This is to me the meaning of life, to take what you have been given, nurture it, and hand it on to the future, and even better to love with all your heart whilst so doing.... I have lived on two continents, and I have been to seven countries by now, I cannot help but ponder the countless days I have lost waiting for a person. Peering into the crowd leaving the subway, waiting so long and coldly, only for reality to finally arrive, the reality that the person I waited for never existed or they have long left the subway. That no one came, and no one intended to know me, it was all just in my head.

Funny how strolling through the deserted park on the first days of September can give you such wild thoughts, making your mind whirl with thoughts like a swirling dervish lost in his own bliss. It is strangely incredible, sad, and a little scary the capacity that silence has to say everything.

***

The hustle and bustle of the street pull me towards the window, so I can witness the flow of life in the noisy and busy city. A street where each of us is looking for an opportunity to escape from its smoke and fumes to a quiet and secluded place, where our body and soul can find peace. Everything is rushing around. People are rushing without looking back. There is an overflow of everything everywhere. With Instagram posts, if you want to keep up, you will have to spend entire days glued to your phone. Books are being written and published at an alarming pace, and I will not even have time to travel with one of them peacefully. My heart aches for myself and the world I was born into. It is a world full of suppressed voices and choked sobs, where bridges to nowhere were built, and hashtags only found resonance in the virtual realm.

Sometimes I feel like I cannot keep up. Or maybe I just want to enjoy what is and experience it deeply instead of rushing to the next thing. Sometimes I just want to hit the brakes and yell,

"Hey, wait, I want to go through this with you too, why are you rushing so fast?

***

Have you ever felt the need for someone's presence? As if you could be happy just standing next to them, in complete silence? Because I have and I still do. I miss someone with whom I have not walked many streets, but, in all my memories, she walks! For the summer that was really summer and never left its role, for the winter that was really winter. For her who spoke less and was the quietest in the group but still existed. A few days ago, I had a dream where she came to say goodbye to me. It was not in some distant future; the sun was shining like it was summer. I remember in my dream I hugged her and cried tears of joy, because the last time we met was nearly two years ago, but she came to spend this last day with me. And it meant everything.

I miss having easy conversations, laughing at someone's jokes with no expectations, no fear of my words sounding wrong, and not walking on eggshells trying to protect everything. I just want to say everything I have to say because my soul is in a lonely place. And now, to exist, I must shout, talk constantly, and talking has become exhausting for me. I do not know how many pages it will take to find myself among my words. I want to share everything that is in my head with someone, but I cannot right now. It is not that there is no one to talk to, the words just will not come out. There are so many thoughts in my head, but none of them want to form into sentences. It is that feeling when you want to say so much, but you just cannot find the words. It overwhelms me and makes me sigh sadly, hiding in the night's silence.

Every evening in recent days, I spend looking at an empty page of my diary or a blank page on my laptop, or an empty note on my phone. The only thing that comes to mind is the thought: "I have nothing to say". I am still drained. It has been over 100 days since I smoked my last cigarette, but that feeling and craving still haunts me. I do not know what to do. Every time I am asked about creativity, I see an image of a balcony, summer, and a smoldering cigarette. Silence and peace. A feeling of loneliness. Due to recent events, I feel it very acutely now and I cannot do anything about it. I hate this. Every time I think it is all resolved, I fall into this endless abyss, it seems like a trauma that I will still have to learn to live with. Although I have almost gotten used to it. I want to shut out everything and not come across any triggers. How tired I am. I only ask that death find me as I am now, without desire, without hope, without dreams.

***

The memory of your love is like a scar on my soul, a pain that never fades and a wound that never heals. I still love you. And you are the only person I would let in time and time again to be a part of my troubles, to be a part of my discomfort, to be a part of my devotion.

To be honest, I realized that I had been wrong to think that I was on equal footing with you. There was no way! You were so golden, so measured, unlike me. I knew that I could never reach your heights in that life. And you know what is funny? I do not even want to. It is much more comfortable for me to be at my depth, at least because there is no need to lie there - many people only look at the external, inflated, lifting their heads and noses up, forgetting that we are all just pieces on a big chessboard. And you, my dear, keep being bold, measuring every breath, recording every step, God forbid if you stray from the plan. And as for me, I have been drawing my own destiny since childhood, and my hand would not shake for anything. My mistake was seeking love where I knew it would only bring me pain. I dove headfirst into our relationship, fearless and heedless of the consequences of such passion, and here I am, losing nights of sleep wondering where you are.

I remembered you today. I thought about how longing did not tear or hurt this time. The yearning now is gentle, grateful, and serene. It does not hurt and does not even make me want to look for you. You were undoubtedly the softest love of my life, but as with all great love, it must come to an end.

My dearest love, my heart is still filled with thoughts of you - wondering if you have found happiness, if you have come to realize that you are worthy of all the good things in life, and if you have stopped belittling yourself. I also often wonder if you still read my words and try to understand my side, and if you can still feel the depth of my love for you. For I still yearn to hold you one last time and disappear with you into a world of our own. My one desire is for you to take care of yourself, to be fearless, and to believe that true love never fades. Be beautiful and happy, my love, but most importantly, be true to yourself. I implore you to read good books, listen to music that moves your soul, and surround yourself with people who lift you higher. Be bold, be daring, if you like, but be kind, too, especially to yourself - kindness is the main decoration of a person. I love you, wherever you are, darling, or whomever you are with.

And as for me, I have felt so much that I no longer know what to feel. I have lost my emotions; I have lost my joy. Now everything is gray, now I am gray. I no longer find meaning in anything; I am merely living by inertia. I have no desire or strength left to keep trying. I carry this great knot in my mind and an immense heaviness in my body, turning my everyday existence into a relentless battle, converting what was once easy into arduous challenges. I only cling to the certainty, born from my own experience, that this moment, sooner or later, shall pass. All I am left with are these words, and they will always be warm to my soul and my heart.

***

From beneath zero, I speak. From the depths of coldness that harbors a strange appetite for swallowing memories. From the abyss of freezing that possesses the skill of shattering the bones of connection.

Is there still no news from the letter?!

I can feel the remnants of the warmth of your laughter in the air here. My heart longs for purposeless wanderings, it drifts away, seeking refuge in the verses that weave the echoes of my melancholy. For sudden embraces that chase away the winter chill. I miss picking flowers, gathering plums from the corner of the courtyard. Does the tranquility there ever get disrupted by the terror of your empty hands? Can I ever glimpse between the harbor, the river, and grand aspirations? Lest the warmth there quench me! The eastern sun always seemed larger to me.

I fear being buried beneath the snow here. I am afraid of the sky, the horizon, and the moon. It is cold here.

Send a little bit of the East to me.

***

Nuremberg, November 25, 2020

The last days of November are always accompanied by a chaotic and violent stream of thoughts. Work, household chores, and preparation for the new year. The routine is unyielding, with no deviation from the expected. It is a dull and monotonous world, the era of spontaneity's silent death. The darkness has crept in, seeping through the cracks of a world consumed by selfishness, greed, and immorality. I am horrified. This world is pressing so hard that I will soon forget how to breathe. As if with every passing year, life becomes more unbearable.

This world is a cold, unforgiving, and heartless place. It is a place of shadows and secrets, of whispered conversations in dark corners. It is a place where the weak are preyed upon and the strong rule supreme. We become cogs in a machine, reduced to mere objects, those of us who refuse to succumb to the bleakness of this world are often left behind, forgotten, and ignored. Those injustices break my heart, that power that others exercise at the expense of others and in favor of oneself, it is hard for me to know that we all tolerate this world full of rules of those who do not love, of those who do not suffer, of those who ignore the crying of children and the silent voice of the elderly. I loathe the fact that I inhabit a world filled with egotistical, corrupt, and mediocre people. It is hard for me to accept this impotence of not being able to change the world.

We live in an era, where packaging erases the content, lies kill the truth, hideousness stains beauty, vice strangles virtue, and greed imprisons generosity. Where hate, ignorance, and violence bury peace, love, and happiness. The illusion of closeness and the connection is but a mirage in this barren wasteland, for we are as distant from one another as the earth is from the sky above. In the past, people would cling to relationships. They would travel miles just to meet their loved ones, they would write letters, and wait months and sometimes years for their letter back. But look at us now! With the mere press of a button, we can communicate instantly, yet even that is too much for us to bear.

People converge on interests. Driven by deception and ambition, our communication is transactional, fleeting, and shallow, for we only reach out when we need something. Our inability to connect with others is not at all commendable. Apathy is not something to be praised. We forget the important details as we mindlessly go through our routine, trapped in a world where we see everything but understand nothing. We have outwardly seen so much that our wide-open eyes become dazzled and blinded. Like those who stare at the sun frequently that they become blind and then spend the rest of life staring with their unseen eyes. We are excessively anxious to speak. Beyond that, we are vastly arrogant with our truths. We have turned to stones, hardened by time, and become more cynical each day. Everything has become machine-type and robotic, almost emotionless, like a well-oiled machine, but devoid of life, dead yet surprisingly moving.

The world shifted, gradually slipping into a bottomless abyss. Muddy in sin and vice, mankind is battling in agony, drowning in endless wars and self-destruction. I am ashamed to be a part of this vicious society, a society of consumption, change of concepts, and lack of conscience. Something has changed dramatically in these long decades. No, the paints are still the same, the canvas painting is still beautiful and confusing, heartwarming music still communes with souls, the awe-inspiring sunsets that light up the sky in shades of pink and orange are still around, fields of wildflowers that dance in the breeze, and snow-capped mountains that reach towards the heavens, the sound of waves crashing on the shore, the rustle of leaves in the wind are all beauties to behold, yet something has changed, and it is not for the better. Something deep inside is covered in mold and rot, poisoning the air around it.

Here is another one loaded into the camp of Time, a hapless soul doomed to wander the halls of eternity, a hall of endless darkness where the line between reality and nightmare blurs into obscurity. You may recognize yourself in it, but not yet. For now, you cling to the illusion of infinity, refusing to heed the whispers of mortality. But pause for a moment and look around. Can you see the difference between the decaying, shapeless mass of bones and flesh and your own frail form, clinging to the surface when you try to spread your wings and fly, struggling to break free from the shackles of your existence? I am petrified to think I may turn into a machine from the accumulated actions and interaction algorithms if I do not gather my senses and think of a way to dissociate myself from our world. Then what better refuge than peace-giving silence in the arms of solitude to do just that?

I wonder how many beautiful flowering buds died for someone to wrap themselves in their fragrant essence, as if in luxurious furs? How many people have gone, seen in their greatness, but remained nameless? How many people died in the oblivion pile in another attempt to surf the surface? The depth of unfathomableness, or maybe just the impossibility to express thoughts in words, crushes every day, turning into endless torture for those seeking wanders, but never reaching. Yes, our Noah is building an arc to escape the deluge, but the emptiness of space will overwhelm even these wanton efforts to escape the wrath of the hands of fate invoked by our own gluttony and sloth.

***

Dearest Olena,

As I sit here alone in the room, the memories of our time together haunt me like a ghost. The echoes of your voice still linger in my ears, the warmth of your embrace still feels so real, and the scent of your perfume still fills the air. As I sit down to write this letter, my heart is heavy with a sense of melancholy that I cannot seem to shake off. There is a weight on my chest that I cannot quite describe, a feeling of sadness and longing that lingers in the depths of my being.

In the darkness of my despair, I am wrapped in my thoughts. The thoughts take away my present and land me somewhere where I feel lost. I sit here with a broken heart and shattered dreams. I feel lost, alone, and abandoned as if I am standing in a raging storm with no shelter in sight. It feels like the world is crashing down around me, I am adrift in a sea of pain and heartache, and I do not know how to find my way back to the shore. I find myself thinking about the past, about all the moments that have slipped through my fingers, and the people who have come and gone from my life. I am left alone to face the void that surrounds me.

The nights are long and cold, and the days seem to stretch on forever. I try to find solace in the memories we shared but fail any time I try. There are so many memories that I cherish, but they are tinged with a bittersweetness that I cannot ignore. Perhaps it is the changing of the seasons or the way the light falls in the late afternoon, but something about this moment feels particularly poignant. It is as if the world is shifting, and I am being swept along with it, unsure of where I will land. The weight of the world seems to bear down on me with every step, crushing my spirit and leaving me feeling numb. Life has been unkind, and the adversity I face feels insurmountable.

I know that this letter may seem somber, but please do not worry about me. I am simply reflecting on the ups and downs of life and trying to make sense of it all. I merely express the overwhelming sadness and heartbreak that I feel. Life is a cruel and unforgiving mistress, unrelenting in her pursuit to test my resolve. She throws curveball after curveball, forcing me to dodge and weave, to keep my footing in a world that is constantly shifting beneath me. Life has taken so much from me. It has robbed me of my loved ones, my childhood, my dreams, my hopes, and my happiness. It has broken my heart repeatedly, and I do not know how much more I can take. It feels like every time I try to pick myself up, life knocks me back down again. The weight of the burden that I carry is too much for me, for my broken heart, for my wounded soul. And life seems to have a never-ending supply of hardships, heartache, and pain. I am standing still but weary and torn from fighting them back, too. The problem I have now is that I try to make sense of the senseless when my senses have long died.

Olena, I am writing this because I am in one of those moments now, battered and bruised by the adversity that has been raining down on me. My heart aches with the weight of loss, and the absence of loved ones who have been taken from me too soon.

My soul is weary from the constant struggle to make ends meet, to keep my head above water in a world that is stacked against me. And my mind is exhausted from the mental gymnastics of trying to find a way out of this maze of hardship. It is hard to keep going when every step I take feels like I am wading through quicksand.

My love, should you also find yourself feeling melancholic, do not hesitate to write to me. If the thorns of despair have taken root in your heart, fear not to unburden yourself to me. For we are in this together, and not all of life's tribulations can be borne alone. Sometimes a few words, a sympathetic ear, the soothing notes of a melody, or a warm hug can help ease the agony. I hope one day soon, the moon will reveal to you how I unveiled myself by writing poetry to you. I hope that someday you can forgive me for whatever wrongs I may have done. I hope that someday, we can find our way back to each other, and once again dance under the stars. But for now, I will simply sit here in the room, holding onto the memories of what we once had and keeping in my memory the beautiful image of your smile as one of my most precious memories.

***

In the world of wizards, all magical items are ordinary, while for us they are amazing. But what if there is magic in our world, too and we overlooked them because we thought of them as "ordinary"? It is just that we are used to it and do not notice it. We do everything on autopilot, losing our taste and sense of smell. We do not feel the roughness of a sweater, the smoothness of keys, or the relief of a doorknob.

Words. This is one type of magic in our world. Well-chosen words can turn into spells that actually work, not just nonsense. Every alchemist dreamed of turning lead into gold, finding the Philosopher's Stone, and achieving immortality. Every writer dreamed of writing a book, becoming famous all over the world, and entering eternity. Twenty-six letters of the English alphabet, and how many words! But mastering magic is hard work, it is not just waving a wand. It takes training. And courage and perseverance. Just like an artist, a writer needs to accept and not be afraid to look foolish. And it will happen, undoubtedly. Writing ten texts. Writing a hundred notes. Catching a thousand small details, looking around. Building up the muscle of imagination, cutting off the excess for the benefit of the main idea. Concentrating the meaning in a metaphor. So that one day, those same words will make goosebumps rise on the skin. They will be remembered. They will pierce. They will awaken that sincere, touching, real thing that lives in each of us.

I will leave. We will all leave someday. The stars have long since gone out, but we still see their light in the vast sky. If I can leave a light that will shine even after hundreds of years, then I will have become an alchemist.

***

Joseph, my dear sibling,

My shattered heart feels as though it may never love again. I do not know if I will. Love is a distant memory, I have lost the strength to believe again, to trust again, to hope again, to require myself to give more than I should expect to receive, to squeeze myself to the limit and shrink to the point of nothingness. To love is a luxury you pay dearly for. I close my eyes and think of every betrayal, every lack of interest, attention, care, and neglect. Every crooked and bloody word stains my heart and sticks into it like a red-hot rod. I think of how I painted smiles on their faces, but they repaid me with tears. How I sowed seeds of hope in their lives, only to reap a harvest of despair in my own. How I bestowed upon them my unyielding trust, only to be stabbed in the back by their betrayal. How my heart bled with an abundance of love, only to be forsaken and left desolate. How they fled, how they walked away, leaving me standing there, a statue of despair, unable to utter a word.

My heart is broken, torn, and not whole. I am a shadow of who I once was. I am on the verge of becoming a broken man or a beast, for sometimes my thoughts fly high beyond the cosmos, while other times I fail to even see my own foot. I have lost my sense of feeling, sometimes I am almost numb, and sometimes storms of feelings. As you delve into my words, I wish for you to grasp the essence of who I am, where I stand, and the musings that occupy my mind. You are receiving the words of a man who has long felt out of place in a society that values conventions and norms that he cannot abide by. Maybe I am made of goodbyes or even loneliness. Maybe I have been alone for so long that I do not know how to love, or rather, how to be loved. Or perhaps, I am too much of an outsider to be understood by those around me. Maybe, I am too far gone in my disillusionment to make any sense of this world.

But I have reached a point where I am unable to envision someone falling in love with me, let alone the idea of them indulging in thoughts of me before retiring for the night, or sharing tales of me with their confidantes, beaming with delight. The notion of someone being swept off their feet by a mere greeting from me or breaking into a smile at the sight of a notification from my end on their phone screen now seems entirely implausible. In truth, I cannot fathom it and perhaps, never could. Sometimes I have the fear that at some point, for some insignificant reason, people will throw me out of their lives in the cruelest and most indifferent way possible.

The other night, as I laid awake in my darkened room, I stumbled upon a line from "A Moveable Feast" by Ernest Hemingway which reads, "We would be together and have our books and at night be warm in bed together with the windows open and the stars bright". The words stirred something deep within me, igniting a longing for such a moment. The thought of two souls entwined, basking in the glory of their love, with the cool night breeze brushing against their skin, and the twinkling stars above them. But do you really feel what is graciously majestical about nights like that? That this could be about two kids in a tree house, a pair of passionate lovers, or a mother and her kids. Those tiny universal moments anyone can have. Anyone can enjoy and share. Whether it is in a luxurious hotel suite or the corridors of a sprawling mansion, love is there.

Yet "love" is too often a game of self-delusion and idealized projections, where we create a world of "shoulds" and "oughts," at the expense of what is. It is a tragedy that so many of us fall in love not with our beloved but with the image we have created of them in our minds. We lose sight of the person before us, caught up in the web of our own delusions. We become blind to the simple truth that there are people with whom you waste your time and then there are others with whom you lose track of time. That there are souls destined to share flowers, but never to create a garden.

***

Nuremberg, October 8, 2020

Have you been alone this week? Truly alone. The kind that leaves you devoid of distractions, not the type when you are mindlessly scrolling through your phone. But when you are completely still and quiet, alone with your thoughts? I have been practicing the art of aloneness, delving into the gift of silence it brings. That silence. The one that allows me to listen to thoughts in the background. The one in which I hear so much more than in the constant flow of words. I slide gently into that chosen solitude, the one that has its own grace, the one that excludes any presence, including mine, not out of ego and arrogance, but out of honesty. The one that is good for me, that I lack nothing, that I am not obliged to occupy myself wondering about the dark thoughts I carry inside. Where I long for lightness because I am exhausted of trying, weary of explaining, of committing myself alone. This lightness guides me to the bittersweet realization that sometimes it is good to let things happen to me. No intervention but mere acceptance.

This Nuremberg wind reminds me of the words of Fernando Pessoa, that great poet of the wind.

"I hear the wind blow, and I feel that it was worth being born just to hear the wind blow."

How true these words ring in my ears as I stand here, mesmerized by the howling gale. Just hearing the wind blow by makes it worth having been born. In my hand, I hold a small espresso, its warmth spreading through me like a comforting embrace. I am in my brother's apartment, and from a nearby window, the sun falls from the shoulders of the sky and sets on the horizon, leaving the remains of a yellow-hot ray on the grass. Silence, the hand of the clock is ticking carefully to measure the time that passes so quickly. I feel the wind and smell the scents brought by the wind. I stand still and watch nature. Focus on color, light, the wind, the air, and the sky. It opens my senses like nothing else.

The scenery here is ever-changing, a canvas that is constantly being painted and re-painted by the capricious hand of nature. In just a few minutes the sky can be soaked in blue and grey, clouds stretching down to touch the ground, and pockets of sunlight revealing streaks of rain-like dust caught in the rays. My mind is a whirlwind of ideas - too many to form into full-fledged stories. I finished one last week and hope to finish another very soon. Though I must admit that I am good at starting things, and not always so good at finishing them. I have spent almost every day here. Thinking. Sitting. Being. And if it is not absolutely freezing, sometimes reading. And each time, an excerpt from "Enough", by Andru Defeye echoes through my mind like a gentle breeze.

"Your simple act of being is enough. Do you see it yet?"

Everything I see has some finesse inherent in an interesting combination with the simplicity of objects. The sky is the portal to calmness. Have always loved and been fascinated with clouds and breathing them in. It is not a surprise that anytime I remotely feel downhearted, I look up to the sky. One of my favorite blessings is when I am looking up and everything becomes perfect and crystal, the air swells and it holds more weight when you breathe it in. Daily reprieve gifted from Nature. Our part is simply being there to pay attention or as Hermann Hesse once said,

"From there on to the fully trained artistic eye is the smaller half of the journey; the principal thing is the beginning, the opening of the eyes."

Nature has a way of silencing me. How could she not, when the intricacy of a single flower, its delicate petals, and vibrant colors are a testament to its wonders? The way a butterfly flutters its wings, dancing through the air with effortless grace, is a marvel to behold. Every place I stand is a new way of experiencing the world. On a clear starry night, going out into the field and looking at the sky - I am humbled by the millions of worlds above my head. It is possible that there are billions of creatures living inside each of them, perhaps similar to me, or perhaps better than me in their circle. Yet sometimes and strangely enough, I do not think being born was worth it at all, but hearing the wind blow makes it worth choosing to stay.

***

It is hard to find the right key. Usually, it is not enough to just hop on a broomstick and zoom ahead in pursuit of "the one". It usually resembles more of a game of cat and mouse or wandering in the fog. Keys are different. Some open the doors to extraordinary adventures, new paths, and undiscovered worlds. Others are escape keys. They lead to an exit, a breath of fresh air and freedom, sometimes revealing previously unknown solutions. Sometimes, instead of opening, they close. They lock up with four bolts, separating what one is trying to escape from. Often, they break, blocking the way back. You can never be sure if you have found the right one. However, until you try to turn the lock, you will not know what is on the other side. Nothing will change. I search for keys. In my hand, the unique pieces of metal jingle, calling out to their cousins. Will they find each other? Where will they lead me?

Somewhere.!

***

You will probably receive this letter in late August. It is extremely hot here. The fruit trees in the orchard have borne fruit, and it seems like an eternal quarrel has arisen between me and other corners of the world. I love to just look at the garden for hours and imagine your enchanting majesty in it. While you look at me from afar, I imagine. I can even feel your footsteps that turn my heart into a field of mythical battles. This is the nature of love that steals the thread of speech from human language and lures anyone into the trap of imagination. The fragrance of your love is the ink of my pen and the friend of my diary. You are the sweetest hallucination. I am ready to go crazy with you and remain insane, beyond the orbits of planets, in the empty space where no one exists but us. How long I searched for you everywhere, on the streets, among people, in poetry and novels. When I go to sleep, I search for you in my dreams, but there is not even a hint. And now I live in the past, like a chewed-up cassette tape, always rewinding. Forever in my memory is your sweet, tired gaze. Like a snowdrop in the spring, a blooming smile. Everything about you is beautiful, as if I am dreaming.

Olena, writing a letter to you has become difficult lately. People here talk about everything, about everything except love. Sometimes I feel the need to distance myself from them all, so far away that I can easily turn to you, to your words, to your hands while drinking tea, and to those few strands of white hair that have recently emerged from sides of my hair. I wish our neighbors would fall in love, so they would consider me less of a secluded madman who has fallen behind in the world. I wish their beloved would be in love with literature and philosophy and tell them about Rumi, Nietzsche, Dostoevsky, and Kafka. I wish you would write me a letter soon, too, and not leave me alone with this strange crowd! You know, we have embarked on this journey together and the common signs of this bond are the continuous letters of love. For love is nothing but a shared sorrow... write to me, tell me who in this city will inform me of your incurable absence? A city trapped in the cancer of despair, soaked in the sea of sorrow, without any savior present to offer a momentary escape from these dark and murky days. Who will bring me news of you? In a city devoid of tender hearts, filled with bitterness and animosity, kneaded with envy, who will guide me on your path when no trace of your affection will remain on my crimson shirt?

My dear, I do not know where in this city and in front of which mirror you are standing. Amidst the restless turmoil, what common letters do your mind think of, and which words are repeated to you over and over again? But write to me, please.

***

Nuremberg, December 5, 2020

The beauty of nature knows no bounds I swear, no end to its splendor. It is a world where life knows no death, where everything is transformed from one form to another. As if nature is not the most prolific storyteller out there! She articulates herself in sediment layers and mountain-top fossils. She whispers her secrets through trodden paths and riverbeds that carve through her bountiful earth. Fresh springs and cascading waterfalls punctuate her sentences, while her rotting branches and hollow tree trunks speak of lives once lived.

These days, I often find myself wandering through Volkspark Dutzendteich. There is something magical about wandering through an old woodland or forest and creeks. To be joined by the breeze, to be caught up in surprise by the wind, to stand and take it all in, to see nature, to hear it, to smell it, to touch it. To sit amidst the trees, to allow the earth to numb your soul and seep into your bones. It is such a blessing, it is a refreshing break from reality, and it is the season to be jolly. To lay down on the grass under a cherry blossom tree, and watch the birds, critters, and clouds. To take a moment and just stand within the trees and breathe. It is amazing to think of the old forests, how they have been there for many generations, and who may have stood in your exact spot or leaned upon the same tree. Thinking about the sunrise poking through the trees, the dew on the grass, the peace. How precious!

> *"And into the forest, I go.*
> *To lose my mind*
> *and*
> *Find my soul."*
> *"John Muir"*

Nature is a boundless wellspring of inspiration, an eternal muse that never fails to surprise and delight me. It all started when I caught myself thinking that I was admiring the fiery hues of autumn leaves and breathing in the crisp, cool air. But then I noticed how the gentle snowflakes danced and twirled their way down to earth, creating a soft, silent wonderland in winter. Yet, as the seasons cycled on and as spring arrived, I watched in awe as everything around me began to awaken and bloom, the air filled with the sweet songs of birds and the scent of fresh greenery. And in the heat of summer, the cool breeze blowing through the trees is a balm for the soul. As time passed, I came to realize that I cherish all seasons for their unique and breathtaking beauty. The road to the pond is surrounded by greenery. The first berries ripened in the garden and were eaten. Fluff flies from poplar trees like snow and settles on the surface of a pond covered with small rowan. The cool breeze from the pond. Dimensional white clouds flying across a clear blue sky. On the way home, I saw all kinds of dragonflies and moths.

In my room, I looked around. The heavy atmosphere of the room fades away under the currents of air. The entire apartment breathes, and the first pages of the book at my feet seem to be animated by the wind's breath. The world is at a standstill, and everything is calm; Under my feet was Atlas: a village in Tatarstan, a river in Cambodia, a mountain range of Africa, and even a star in the constellation Taurus, a satellite of Saturn, and a crater on the visible side of the moon. Everything under my feet: A collection of maps, tables, charts, breathed, pierced, muted, silenced by me for years now. A face without a shape, a shadow without color, a gesture without motion. The years lost to the sands of time. Let those who walked over it all remember like rats on the broken glass of a window - if they remember, they will know what our bodily eyes can detect, an unforgivable mistake. Much needs to be demolished, much built, and much rebirth. Do not spare hands and time, enough of it is wasted.

***

To the one who holds my heart, Olena Petrovych,

It was in those days of Wroclaw when the cold was biting into our very skin, standing by the Odra River, near my dormitory, at the end of every weekend. Talking about what we had for the week. Classes we took, the exams we had, the people we met, the music we listened to, and the movies we watched. Those were the days when the sole background music to our conversations was the rippling of the water, the chirping of the birds, the cathedral bill of St. John the Baptist, and the crunch of the gravel beneath us. When each gesture, each stolen glance, every hug held on a little tighter for a split second longer, felt just a little bit more, but never quite enough.

I never thought I would write a letter to you again. But you know, the beauty of life lies in its unexpectedness. Believe me, if I ever think for a moment that everything is just the way it is, I will no longer want to continue this life. The beauty of life is that her black is not always black, and her white is not always white. Her existence is not eternal, and every day that I live, my eagerness to see these inconsistencies increases.

Olena, I wonder if you have ever wondered what would have happened if things had been different. Because I do, and I have imagined different scenarios. We would probably be together, with ups and downs, but with a lot of love involved. There is also the possibility that we did not last long and that everything ended as quickly as it began. Or maybe we would never have gotten anywhere and all we would have been a bitter taste from our failed attempt. We could never know the answer. And now only particles are left in the air, some of which are tiny fragments of you. These fragments sway along with the wind, moving to the rhythm of my nostalgic breaths. At times, I find myself conversing with you in the past, from the time when we were once inseparable, and I can remember all the hugs and cups of steaming coffee that we left in the care of an "after" that never came to fruition.

Honestly, there will always be a part of me that feels a thousand things about you. If only my life could transcend all boundaries and distances, I would have spent it wandering the universe of my heart, seeking memories we shared and those we could have had. If I had known that our last hug was going to be the last, I would not have let go. If I had known that our last hangout at the coffee shop was going to be the last time, then I would have begged God to stop the time and allow us to enjoy that moment. It was worth it just to be there looking at you and telling myself how much I loved you. For I loved you in a way no poets have ever written poems about it and no Parisian lover has ever felt it. And if one day you healed, and if when you healed you still loved me, look for me, I will have healed too and maybe I will still love you. And if you do not, that is fine. I just hope you are doing well, and doing what's right for you, after all, on my part we were just two people knowing what "love" is.

***

My beloved brother Joseph,

How can I even explain what I think of our world? I think the greatest failure of humans is the genuine fear many people have of being alone with their thoughts for longer than five minutes. Some of the greatest conversations I have ever had were the ones I had with myself, with the darkest corners of my own mind. I see we package our loneliness in the sunniest smiles, only to return home and feel like the emptiest beings in the universe. A little laughter, a little noise, a little frivolity, and feigned confidence - the perfect container for absolutely nothing. We are all missing pieces of our souls, and we yearn to be whole again. These soul mates, friends, and family, all fill in a piece. You ache for the biggest piece. We are looking for warmth, like newly born puppies, blindly poking into other people's palms, naively trying to predict - will they hit? pat? play and leave? They will take pity on us, give us shelter, put us on our feet, and then, smiling frivolously, slam the door behind us.

I am starting to see that no one owes anything to anyone, but everyone is somehow childishly waiting for something from each other. Cautiously reaching for warmth, fearfully sharing it, becoming attached and tying, abandoning, and remaining abandoned - this happens. Sometimes this love we have is enough for two, sometimes for a dozen, and sometimes this love is not even enough for oneself. We pack our loneliness in love and sympathy, putting all the fears, all the pain, and all the longing that is in the package, we close the box tightly and solemnly hand it over to the first person who asks for help. Nothing wears me out with a person more than to see them hand their day and their lives to the other person and say, "Go ahead, ruin my day." It is of course not a threat or a warning, it is an absolute invitation.

How I yearn for my eyes to witness only the beauty that this world has to offer. To be oblivious to the darkness that pervades the earth, and instead relish the darkness that adorns the night skies. But alas, we have been cursed to behold the shadows that loom over our existence, and in turn, have forgotten the radiance of the stars above. These eyes only see tiredness, suffering, and sadness these days. Being closed is a pain and being open is another pain. You cannot imagine the amount of pain that hovers in my soul, which has penetrated every bone of mine. My soul is like those who have gone mad with grief and are beginning to laugh. I think my only desire from this world is for there to be silence until everything calms down, so that the voice of my mind can scream loudly in my head, saying, "Be patient! Everything can get worse than this." Then I become certain that living through bad moments and witnessing even worse moments is possible. I want to keep silence by my side to the extent that when people die, silence dies with me. It fades away from the crowd's commotion and peacefully rests in the corner of the room, on the left side, behind the yellow couch.

There is not much that I fear in this world if anything at all. But I dread the prospect of becoming like the people around me. A stranger to myself, yet a familiar face to the rest of the world.

I always feel like I am standing on one side of the world, with the rest of humanity on the other. I am terrified of the prospect of crossing over to their side, of becoming just another face in the crowd. I fear that day when while crossing the street, I witness a moment where my true self clashes with my fabricated self, they stare at each other, shocked and speechless, before asking the cutting question: "Why do you pretend to be someone you are not?" For the only thing worse than being alone in this world is losing oneself in the masses.

***

Now that I am writing to you, you are far away. You are sitting in a cafe, reading your favorite book. I guess you order your tea around 3 pm today, just like every other holiday. Unlike me, who always frowns with great concentration, you look at the words of the book completely indifferent, and even with the strange events that happen in the book, your eyebrows do not raise, or like me, when the plot suddenly changes and twists, you do not quickly change your sitting position. I am sure you get impatient from the absence of a single table in the cafe and reluctantly sit at a table with two chairs facing each other, and sometimes your gaze falls on the empty chair in front of you, and you start thinking about splitting the table in half!

I read somewhere that silence between two people brings them closer, so I think if I happen to see you completely unexpectedly in the cafe and we sit face to face, we would be very close! Honestly, you are the only person I desire that only my eyes speak to, and perhaps the only person I try not to be too talkative around, so I can hear your voice more, the sound of your vocal cords and maybe, compared to that, the sound of your eyes... You were just like a dream, when I would seek refuge in bed, more tired than ever. You were the pleasant scent of narcissus, gently wafting towards my face. You were the delightful spring breeze amidst the apple trees, a moment of breath in the air untainted by the world's pollution. You were the sole reason for my return, to revisit memories, the only definitive decision I made throughout these years, and the last remaining fragment of hope from the past year.

***

As I strolled down the street, my gaze fell upon a dim and gloomy café. The sign was worn, and the window appeared lackluster. Its walls were uneven, and the roof was slightly askew. The open door lured me in, and I found a tiny circular table outside with two iron chairs, just large enough to hold two glasses of wine.

It was a diminutive cafe, intimate and human in its proportion. I could not help but feel drawn to it. There was something about its size and imperfections that made me feel at ease as if I could sit there without judgment. It had beautiful old cups that were lightly chipped and cracked, a sign that one should appreciate life's imperfections, a metaphor for one's own fragility, and a reminder to be gentle. It was a place where I could be myself, without worrying about my appearance or how the world perceives me. Perhaps it was the scars of intense living that drew me to this cafe. The wear and tears of life had softened me, making me appreciate the beauty in imperfection. It was a proper setting for a human being, a place where I could connect with others on a human level and feel open to all the emotions that flowed from it. The weight of beauty can be a heavy burden to bear.

Each day, my eyes are opened to more and more of the world's splendor, and the sheer magnitude of it threatens to overwhelm me. There is so much I long to do, so much I ache to experience, that my mind feels as though it might split open from the pressure. It is a maddening sensation, this insatiable hunger for life, for art, for everything that makes this existence worthwhile. But I would not have it any other way. To feel so alive, to be consumed by the passion and the pain of living is a privilege that not everyone is granted. And so, I embrace the madness, the chaos, the endless possibilities. For what is life without a little madness?

***

Dear Joseph, my trusted confidant,

As much as I despised it, I found myself enamored with her beyond measure. I had no intention of surrendering myself as a slave to her love, yet here I was, consumed by the scorching flames of love whenever she was not by my side. Do not misunderstand me, brother, her existence alone was a source of great joy for me, but the emptiness I felt when she was away was unbearable. All of a sudden, she became the air I breathed. and I found myself longing to hold her hands, to connect with the child still alive within her. I yearned to wander through the world inside her mind and see what my definition is. From the outset, I knew that our friendship would be enchanting and bring us both immense happiness. Yet, I also knew that it was destined to come to an end. I knew that my love for her would eventually be the cause of its demise, crushing my heart in the process. I knew all of this, and yet, I could not help but feel regret for possessing such a weak heart.

But can you blame me for such profound love that has burrowed its way into my heart for her? I was feeling the gentle rhythm of her breath, the scent of her hair, and the captivating look on her face when I was listening to her. Her closeness to me felt tangible as if the very air was charged with her presence. Even now, as reality cruelly reminds me of the distance between us, I still sense her by my side. The ray of sun that illuminated her face, has long since faded, but the warmth of her memory lingers on, and my heart aches for her.

My dear brother, the conclusion we reached has left me shattered, utterly and completely. The finality of our parting words, the end of our last farewell, it felt as if a piece of me was lost forevermore. All the light, the love, and the rapture this world had to offer vanished in an instant. I will feign indifference, claiming that her thoughts and feelings hold no sway over me, but it is a lie. The truth is that I cannot forget her, no matter how hard I try. She remains in the forefront of my mind, forever etched within my heart. It is a daunting task to get someone out of your life who has not even come out of your mind, much less from your heart. How does one move on when their heart still beats with the unyielding passion of a love that refuses to die? Oh, the agony of unrequited love! It is a curse that I shall carry until the end of my days.

Am I descending into madness to admit that I still speak to her in my mind? Engaging in lengthy, profound discussions about life, philosophy, literature, and our written works. Perhaps it is the memories of what I once had that I yearn for. Memories of her footsteps fading into the floral fields, under a pure blue sky, and pure white clouds, the wind fluttering the petals around her, and the birds chanting their recitals. Perhaps this scene is nothing more than a painter's canvas giving color to his desires, or a poet's poem reviving nostalgia for his muse. Sorry, I am not trying to be pretentious. I am simply trying to recapture the hues that have faded from memory. I long to distinguish between the fiery red of her lips and the blood that spills from wounds. I want to discern the white of her smile and the blank stare of my shattered mind. I want to remember the beautiful blue of her dress and feel its stark contrast to the garment that slowly fades to a somber hue in moments of defeat. I want to see again all those colors impregnated in the petals that shake in the air because of the wind, while I search to find her footprints on floral fields again.

I miss the husky timber of her voice, the smoky notes that lingered in the air. I miss the sound of her laughter, the way it echoed through my soul. But most of all, I miss the comfort of knowing she was near. The assurance that she was just a breath away, a mere heartbeat from my grasp. I miss the anticipation of seeing her every day, the certainty of her presence, be it on a lazy Saturday afternoon, a tranquil Sunday morning, or a mundane Monday evening.

But alas, such thoughts have been shattered by a harsh reality. Now, I find myself lost in a deep, crippling numbness. As if my heart has chosen to shut down and ceased to feel since our last encounter. I am convinced that there must exist a word, a phrase, or some elusive expression that could adequately convey the depths of what I feel. A mean to demonstrate to you, to her, and to the world, what I am harboring within that keeps me perpetually silent. If such a thing does not exist, then perhaps this world that I inhabit is not meant for me. In that case, my only recourse is to flee, to hasten my steps and leave all behind, without ever looking back. For it appears that I may only find safety in some distance elsewhere, far from the confines of this bleak and unyielding reality.

***

Dear Olena,

If you had heard my side of the story or if you had only seen the sparkle in my eyes when I was talking about you, perhaps you would have stayed a bit longer! I am no longer worried about whether we are going to get passed all the "ifs" and "buts" and meet again, I have made peace with that. My soul longs for you and life have proven to me that nothing lasts forever. That the universe does not halt in mourning for our grief, and I have grown accustomed to this void and agony in my life, but it irks me to reiterate that no one deserves to fall asleep and wonder why they were not enough.

At times, I wondered if my love for you was a sin that required forgiveness. But what else could I have done? I fled the city for weeks, seeking to escape your memory, but soon I failed. I left the country and deserted the squares, streets, and places where our memories live. I tried to escape but soon, I ended up facing the truth! That nothing has changed, nothing has vanished except my poor soul. I was worried that the thought of you and your memories would keep chasing me to my very last breath, chaining me to their never-ending grip. I was afraid that the ship of my thinking would sink into the ocean of your love, leaving me to drown in its unfathomable depths.

But the bird has flown, and the ship has sailed, love has changed me now. I thought at the time that it bruised me only much later to realize that it was me hurting myself. It took me some time to understand what love truly means. Love does not require a happy ending. It just needs to be. Love is a value on its own. It crushed me for years until I learned to appreciate love itself without attaching it to the need to physically be close to the loved one. And I guess that is eternal love. It does not disappear, does not leave, or stop existing. It is always there. It is like looking into a mirror wherein our eyes see the love within love and more of love. Endless images twirling and merging one into another like the skirt of a dancing dervish.

Love is the beauty and embellishment of this universe. Love exists. Just not in the form in which they are used to presenting it. Love lives in respect, in acceptance. It is in the work we love, in the place where we live, in the blanket with which we hide, in the book to which we return again and again. This feeling lives in such things that we tremblingly protect. It is a lack of love which turns the homes into barren deserts; which fills the heart with the trash of grudges and malice; which takes away the peaceful sleep and laughter of friendship. Love makes you see things in different ways. It makes the strange streets in foreign countries homes for lovers. It makes a home out of the arms of strangers. Love upon its arrival kisses you like you are dew in the morning and touches you like you are a museum artifact. Otherwise, what makes our world precious? What gives value to our gaze, our steps, and our hands? What enriches the wealth of our souls? What forms the foundation of all that is beautiful? What can captivate all the intellectual foundations of a person? Truly, what is it, if not the miracle of love? How fortunate can a person be to fall in love?

The only thing that matters to me now is to know that you are taking care of yourself and that you are loved. In my heart, I hold onto the hope that you are smiling while drinking your tea at our favorite coffee shop or traveling across cities in your dream Volkswagen car. I retain the hope that you put on your red lipstick, wear your floral midi peasant skirt, and tie a scarf around your neck, lighting a cigarette before the grand entrance of the University, as if this world is all yours and you are warmed with love. That is all that matters to me now, for I vow to love you my lifetime, if that is all in life I ever do.

***

It was four-thirty in the morning, amidst fever and tremors, I was delirious. I do not remember what delusions I had; I only remember that there were two of us. One person, curled up like patients in a movie, was sweating and trembling, uttering delirious words. And another person, calm and indifferent, was listening to the words of the former and stifling laughter.

Many times, I have longed to be two people. One who brings relief, who offers a glass of water and says everything will be fine. One who gets angry, one who, like my dear old friend who keeps me sane, places his hands on both sides of my face and says, "Calm down, my friend, calm down." One who is fearless and embarks on any unfamiliar path. One who is wise and appears to bring me peace and tranquility. One who is free, one who remembers that there is always a chain around the foot of the dove. One who is loved, and one who keeps an eye on them and constantly reminds them to savor each second, as parting is on its way.

It was four-thirty in the morning. My home was the sea, and the bed was a broken boat. I, twisted like a fearful and trembling prophet from the signs revealed to him, were two people. One person was uttering delusions, and his words were so absurd that the other person burst into laughter.

Then, the sun rose, and the two of me slowly intertwined, and my shadow merged with the wall.

The fever was gone, the storm was gone, and I remained... Just like always!

***

Dear Brother Joseph,

The world is a bleak and melancholic place, a vast expanse of emptiness and solitude, a somber landscape of gray skies and empty streets. It is a place where sadness and despair reign, where the weight of the world seems to crush down upon us, crushing it with the enormity of its burdens and leaving us gasping for breath. It is a place where the light seems to have faded, leaving only shadows and darkness behind. A place where hope seems to be just out of reach, where every glimmer of light is quickly snuffed out. We find ourselves lost in our own thoughts, trapped in a spiral of negativity and self-doubt. A place where the sun had disappeared, leaving behind a cold and colorless world.

The wind howled a mournful sound that echoed through the empty alleys and abandoned buildings. This city was once a bustling metropolis, a place of life and energy. But now it is a ghost town, the remnants of its former glory now faded and forgotten. The buildings stand tall and imposing, but they are nothing more than hollow shells, their windows are shattered, and their walls are crumbling. The people who lived in this city are worn down by the weight of their own existence, their faces etched with lines of worry and despair. They moved through their days like ghosts, their footsteps echoing hollowly on the pavement. They spoke in hushed tones; their voices were muted by the weight of their own grief. Most of these people are long gone, leaving behind only their memories and their sorrows. They had fled in search of a better life, leaving behind a world that had failed them. A world that had betrayed their hopes and dreams.

The city streets are empty, safe for the occasional stray dog or cat. They roam the desolate landscape, searching for food and shelter. They are the only living beings left in this desolate place, the only ones who have not given up hope. The sky is a murky shade of gray, a color that matched the desolation of the world below. The clouds hung low, heavy with rain that refuses to fall. It is as if the world is holding its breath, waiting for something to happen. Waiting for a miracle that would bring back the life that had once been. But there is no miracle, no happy ending to this story. The world remains a bleak and melancholic place, a place of sadness and sorrow. A place where dreams die, and hope is nothing more than a distant memory.

In this city, the world seems to be bathed in an everlasting grayness, the sky an endless expanse of dark, dreary clouds. The air is thick with a damp chill that seems to seep into the very bones of those who dare venture outside. The trees are stripped bare, their branches reaching out like skeletal fingers clawing at the heavens. There is a pervasive sense of loneliness that hangs in the air, a feeling of isolation that seems to permeate every corner of the landscape.

My dear brother, these words may come as a shock to you. Even I, in my darkest thoughts, never thought I would pen such a sorrowful letter. Alas, my heart is shattered! I implore you, do not share these words with our mother. Instead, give her a kiss and reassure her that I yearn for her presence, oh so deeply.

***

I love getting up early with the sunrise. There is some kind of magic in it, some kind of incomparable magic of the atmosphere when the sun just comes into its own and gives its first rays after the unsightly darkness of the night. I revel in waking up early with the sunrise at 5 or 6 in the morning, when the whole city is still lost in slumber. The world outside my window is silent, except for the sweet chirping of birds. I take "The Painted Veil" book and go out onto the balcony, where there is an easy chair, inviting me into its arms. I sit down and immerse myself in the world of the book, while the kettle is boiling in the kitchen. Even after all these years, I still find it hard to see myself belonging anywhere in this world. It has really been a struggle, a lifetime challenge for me to kind of see where I belong. But whenever I read a book or some lines of poetry, I automatically see where I belong; between two pages of a book, between the spaces of two words, between a writer's pen and a paper's line, between the crazy wild waves of poet's feelings and emotions, between the outside silence of a writer and the chaotic world in his head. Yes, it is where I belong.

As the sun began to ascend on the horizon, painting the sky in hues of gold and crimson, memories of your love floods my mind. Your voice, once so clear, has faded into a distant whisper, and your smile, once so bright, is now just a faint memory. Yet your love is still occupying my heart, like a flame that refuses to be extinguished. I convinced myself that it was you who sent the soft, gentle winds that caressed my skin, whispering from a far-off place that you were fine.

Regrets gnaws at my soul like a relentless hunger. I regret not having spent more time with you when I could; of not having hugged you more than I should, of not having given you the attention you so deserved, of not having shown you what I really felt and still feel for you. Those days, I felt like I was drowning in a fast-flowing river! I disagreed with many things in my daily life, but I chose to remain quiet in order to maintain the balance in my life. I wanted to scream, but instead, I bottled it all up, nodded my head, and kept at it. Oh, how I longed to let out a gut-wrenching scream, to express the love that burgeoned within me. I should have been braver and louder in expressing the love I had for you. I should have been more stubborn, insisting what I had and felt towards you was real. I should have been brave enough to walk straight to you and tell you what you mean to me. These are some of the "small" things that require courage.

I believe you needed more bravery, too. You know I usually re-read our old messages and writings. I try to get more meanings from them to know you better. I seriously think you were afraid. Of me, of us, and everything in between. Was I overwhelming and thereby hard to handle? Was I so difficult to understand? You may say no, but even so, I will choose to believe in my gut. I feel like you just ran away because you did not know how to deal with me and the love, I brought you.

I know I am not the person to want things for myself, nor to do things for myself, be it out of will, love, or spite. I am not one to ask for things, to crave something so badly, to demand, to claim as mine. But when it came to you, I wanted you. I wanted you for myself, out of love, will, and spite. You were my only hope. Your existence and your world were a ray of hope that could save me from drowning in despair. For me, you were that desired morning that I never wanted to see set.

And I admit that I am neither used to having people who can understand me, nor I am used to having people to stay with me. I have always lived with this thought, and it had cost me dearly. And I do not know how to put it for you, some feelings are difficult to talk about but let me sum it up all into one sentence, you could have gotten rid of all the layers of dust on my doubts and "what-ifs" in one sentence, "until we meet again". You were everything I wanted but everything I could not have. Yet like a soldier mending his wounds, I was still smiling and looking for victory in your eyes, knowing all along that there were battles I could never win without you by my side. I have said many times that when my eyes were filled with your love, it was as if Ferhad had fallen into the mountain for Shirin's sake. And now, when in turmoil and restlessness, it is as if Persepolis is burning in flames. I found you just like a lost soldier finds his homeland, and a passionate revolutionary finds his dreams.

I now look for unframed smiles in the forbidden attic of things we never talked about and left forgotten in the dust of what one day we wanted to be and never could. I look for smiles in the streets, in photographs, in chats, I look for smiles on the other side of the world connected by the internet. But the world is empty. The world stopped smiling and hiding behind grimaces complicity between two individuals. Condemned to walk with a withered heart, with a sad look, between the fear of being who I am and what I want others to see in me. I do not feel where I should, nor how I should, much less where I would like to be. For a long time, I have been hidden between trapped tears and the sadness that frames a look that hardly anyone sees. I am no longer what I used to be, but I am not what I want to be either. Today I am a dust of someone I once was. It scares me to realize that cities have come between us, and we will never meet. Even coincidences will not be able to bring us together. It scares me to think that maybe one of us will die, and the other will never know! I also need more bravery, at least enough to tell you about these feelings in person. But I do not dare to, and so, I pour my heart out onto these pages, a pathetic attempt to bridge the divide between us, a desperate plea for a miracle to appear and bring you here.

***

I miss the eastern-southern light dancing on the walls with shadows, inviting me to a walk in the nearby parks. I miss her cold embankment and marble columns, the bends of her rivers, and fairy-tale palaces. I fell to the floor. I flew in the clouds, my thoughts were full of something else, obviously not lessons. Another bout of melancholy and despair for no reason. Life force is gone. I silently go to the window and open it, a stream of fresh air rushes into the room. Too lazy to go somewhere. And no one is calling today. I wanted to have everything closer. And I do. Yet at the same time, I have nothing. Neither nature nor freedom. The day closes in "four walls". Wake up, work, feed my body, tide up, go to sleep.

When I wanted things closer, I forgot how the wonderful system of eight-hour workdays drains the entire living day out of life. When it ends, there is no sun left, everything falls silent, closes, and goes deaf. There's no time for getting closer. And soothing nature is farther than ever before. And the calming nature is further away than ever before.

I miss going further. Further used to mean freedom.

***

I am at the most vulnerable point of my life. My body is not enough to accompany you, my pride is not enough to speak it. I have it tied in a knot on my chest, tensing with care, the little that I can discern between the folds of my body. Nor do I break my head when writing to you, it flows over the extinct flows as if it were the last gasp of a dying breath. I am devoid of enough air to finish my sighs. My memory is not enough to hold onto yours. Do not mistake my love for something weak, for I loved you in every letter and of the many poems that the joy of writing did not let me finish. I would have liked to finish them all, but I was not able to let go of the smile that constantly prevented me from communicating my impatience. And that one letter which you chose never to pen to me. I find myself compelled to write answers to its empty void.

Yesterday, I spent the entire day in an overwhelming madness, the entire day in a place among all the devastating ruins! Isolation can darken a person's world. Dark, like death. I wanted to write you a letter and tell you about the confused thoughts and feelings that weigh on my soul like a massive stone, pressing down on me and turning my head into a great whirlwind. I wanted to see you somewhere amidst this dust and join you with the hands of a new beginning. My love, write me a letter and tell me that you will meet me in the midst of these uncertainties. Write and strike a stone of longing, made of the material of yearning.

And as for today, I offer you my current, real, and absent language of love. My heart is with fear that you fed without realizing it. The high degree of sensitivity that takes over my actions and the shaky walk that you never knew how to accompany. Protecting in my chest the pain you caused me and the sadness of accepting it is not enough for me to pay the oblivion quota that you have marked on our attempt to flee, nor accumulate everything I collected on my skin, nor sell all my poems. I have not forgotten your name, but the image of you is fading away from my mind. I fear that one day, all that will remain of you is a mere name - a name that I know, but its face no longer comes back to me. A name that was once familiar to my soul, but now it is just a name. I am afraid you will leave my imagination forever; I fear that my imagination will betray me, stealing away the image of your face, the sound of your voice, and the warmth of your smile forever.

As I sit here writing, I look at the sky and in the leaden gray of the clouds I look for a glimmer of blue and I find it. It is small, it is subtle, it is shy, but it is there. That corner of blue does not know it, but that is all that matters. I am writing confessions again and I will spend the whole night thinking about you. I cannot contain this raging rage and the flow of salty tears. I focus on the colored spots that double in my eyes, as bright as you but fading just as quickly. I want to go back to the time when you said you loved me, when you put your soul, life, and heart in the palms of my hands. When you loved me and made it known.

This heart of mine yearns for something lately, perhaps something my soul remembers that I have forgotten. This yearning brings peace to my mind but leaves my heart heavy and aching. I feel like something is missing and that I want to go back home. The only thing is that I am already home. Then why do I keep yearning for something that my heart feels as home? I fail to understand what the yearning is about. It is like the drop wants to dissolve in the ocean once again, the jigsaw piece wants to be placed back where it originally was. I clung to my feelings for you because they were a breath of fresh air in the midst of apathy and constant anxiety. My love, I think I put too much of myself into you. I guess someone always must love harder. and I am sorry that is me. Late at night, while you sleep peacefully, I sit and find lost pieces of myself.

My problem is that I do not know how it is possible not to love completely. I give my heart away so quickly, even if it leaves a whole hole in my chest, that is because I am haunted by the thought that If I do not hurry to give my heart to those I love, life will snatch them away from my grasp. It has already stolen from me those who were dearest to my heart, a cruel and unfeeling hand that plucks away those I love with no regard for my pain. Each loss pushes me further back in the line, where only the empty comfort of solitude awaits.

I wonder where you will be now. I remember I left you on the sidewalk one night in June and I never saw you again afterward. And if you want, you can look for me. You will find me where there are winds and people do not come close. Where the sky has clouds full of rain, but you can see a bit of blue. Or where you think I should be.

***

Dear love, Olena,

In anticipation of my complaints in this letter, I humbly request forgiveness from you. This letter is filled with complaints, but not towards you. May God silence my tongue if I ever intend to complain about you, as everything I have seen from you has been nothing but goodness and kindness. If only you could see the utter chaos that ravages my soul, the wretched thoughts that torment me, and the profound numbness that pervades my very being, you would feel pity and offer a hug. I feel so alone. Alone at the mercy of many calamities waiting like a pack of ravenous wolves to come upon my poor heart. My heart is burdened by the company of those whose minds are as small as a chickpea and whose mouths are as vast as a cave, constantly interrogating others. They ask so much that one would think their blank minds have yet to form a single thought. I do not believe these people know anything about my world, my dreams, my thoughts, and my worries.

I feel so distanced from myself and the world that dances madly around me. I feel so distanced from that which they call "reality" and I tend to call it "man-made hypocrisy". Though I know I should take pride in my distance from their shallow world, the feeling of being left out that ensues is a formidable foe. I build brick walls around myself; they are not to keep me out but to see who will scale it. Who will put in the effort? I despise the fact that

I have become someone who requires proof of others' intentions, but I realized people take from us until we are empty, and we need to break away to refill. I am not in a favorable state. I feel like I am fading away in a mass of darkness.

It is the middle of the night, and silence is around, fears and sneaky doubts are biting my ankles, and yet I am wearing the thickest socks I have. My remnant in time dies of nostalgia, it comes to me every day whispering the fears that enter me as thoughts and are buried in the deepest way possible; I have told myself to be stronger and block them out, but my awake ears cannot stop listening to the dejected, even less if they recognize the melody of my own crying. I become an ocean looking to one day be a cloud, but I always end up becoming sand or sometimes fire. I cannot help but ponder whether this strange symbiosis is a mere coincidence or a product of some grand design.

My thoughts weaken me. I am no stranger to sleepless nights and tear-soaked pillows. My legs tremble, the silence breaks me, and the emotions I have bottled up for too long now threaten to burst forth from within me. I can no longer bear to be patient, nor do I want to force myself to tolerate the intolerable. I want to stop blaming myself, I want to shout that I cannot, and stop demanding myself. I want to unleash my anger, to deny, to answer, to claim. I want to surprise the doubt with thousand answers, I want to speak until there is nothing else in my throat, in my head, on my chest. I want to dance, jump, run, and move, in all directions and for no reason at all. I want to shake off my sadness. I want to pound on the door of my soul and love myself fiercely every single day.

I want hope. I want to understand myself. I need an unbearable faith that does not fit me in life, I need a firmness that terrifies my fear, my absences, the lack that turned into a ball on the tip of my tongue. I want to disappear into my dreams, dissolve into the abyss of illusions. I want to dive into this thick, foul-smelling jelly. Drowning there from dawn to dusk and not seeing the world behind the dense glass of rose windows. I want to escape reality. My heart hurts, and my soul suffocates from the dust that lies on every day I live. It is unbearable. Build me a house, I beg of you, where I can hide from this cold, from the pain and fear that haunts me every night. I want to fall asleep in a cozy armchair by the fireplace and not be afraid of the open windows through which my anxieties roam like silhouettes.

Yet I feel I lost all intention of saving myself from my own judgment, and in the face of all my insecurities, I plead guilty to every crime my mind whispered to the hatred I had committed. I accuse my will of abandoning me for no reason, and although I would have loved to forgive myself, my errors make me understand that my will is the last thing I could depend on when everything begins to fall. I reproach my bravery for its recklessness and distancing myself from all those who dared to resist my vague decision to let myself win. I cry for myself, for abandoning myself in the midst of it all. I feel regret and remorse for that old me, for my cowardice in not making an appearance when I needed it from myself and when it was required because in the middle of the trial, bravery was named, and silence spoke for both of us.

***

My precious Olena Petrovych,

In the last couple of weeks before leaving Wroclaw, I have been walking as much as my feet can and time allows, taking pictures of all the details and trifles that catch the eye. Each step I took felt heavier than the last as if the very pavement was trying to keep me there. I am already beginning to miss this place, even though I have not yet departed. I will miss this city, and I love this city, as tired as I am. I am going to miss the conversations I often had with strangers in the middle of the street, on the buses, and at cafes. I do not think I will ever forget them - neither their gestures, nor their puzzling looks, nor my whining with a cheeky smile, nor the words that seem meaningless at first, but the longer I think about them, the clearer I realize that strangers are telling me about the most important things. As if they are being set up!

After all, what could be better than memories? Only the realization that it all happened to me, that I walked through these streets, enjoyed the beauty of the architecture, breathed in its grace, and inhaled the smell of history, felt the crunch of snow beneath my boots. Outside, the winter persists, the same season that once filled me with hope. But after long walks under fluffy flakes, yellow streetlights, and the satisfying crunch of snow underfoot, I returned home with a smile and a blush on my face - two signs of a charged soul that bloomed like a rosebud.

Here is some charm in the medieval streets and corners of The Rynek we Wrocławiu. Every bridge stone, every wall of the house, the howling door carving, the old town hall in the square - froze in the indifferent contemplation of today. Maybe buildings have memories too, because every time I see old architecture, I become filled with strange emotions that become more tangible when I touch them; It is as if I am standing on a spot where someone stood before, shedding tears or maybe laughing, perhaps they were confused and bewildered, looking for a way to escape. Tourists are snoozing, merchants are clapping, businessmen are driving beautiful cars – it is all a fuss. I had no chance not to fall in love with this city when it shamelessly revealed its beauty to me with its sunrises and sunsets by the Grunwald Bridge; The noisy subway trains that I rode with a book clutched in my hand; the escalator stairs where you and I embraced before Christmas Eve; the cabin with cherry blossom in Szczytnicki Park; Hotel Sofia near Wrocław Główny, a haven for two hearts in love; golden trees and rustling leaves under our feet; a large pile of books (especially Henryk Sienkiewicz's novel "In Desert and Wilderness", on the first page of which was signed "the most beautiful girl in the world"); flowers on the windowsill: pinkish succulents, and violets; there are many things we left in Wroclaw but the memories are with me.

This is the city where I dropped my heart into the roaring waters of the Odra River. And I have no desire to catch him. This is the city in which I first experienced the true, profound meaning of the word "to live", with all its immense, indomitable power. A city in which I remembered what it is like to live. This is the city in which I walked, as without skin - infinitely vulnerable and susceptible to its eternal beauty, its majesty. The city in which I was not ashamed to cry.

I want to believe in magic. Rejoice in the snowflakes smoothly flying from the sky, gaze upon the mesmerizing lights of the city, and hope that Santa Claus will visit me in the dead of night with a gift beneath the Christmas tree. After all, I fell in love with this city, or you, or both of you together, and I wonder how many hearts you both have stolen. Mine did not last. This is the city I do not get tired of returning to. And I will be back again, I just hope this whole nightmare will end soon. Returning to Wroclaw is not just a return to a city, it is a return to the world's best sunsets, the Odra River, and you.

***

"Life is a train and the people we love are the stations where we decide to stay",

he mused, his cloak of sadness draped around him like a second skin, mere days before his untimely disappearance. He was one of those who sailed turbulent oceans of anguish. One of those who, with smiles immersed in despair, would jump into deep waters to drown just to save the smile of those who needed it most. He was the kind of person who would wait for you until you tied your shoes, while the world moved on without you. He loved the stars and moon, he had said once to me that the more distant, the more beautiful, defining how unattainable the dream life is for many.

He was sad when they did not dance with him to his favorite song, yet he would give them those hugs that save lives. He told me that as long as he could breathe, he would smile and dance as if life were only to be happy. Depression was taking him lately, as a whirlwind takes the most beautiful and largest ship, his smile stopped shining, and he began to fade very dimly. He had dark circles under his eyes from lack of sleep and a pale complexion from being in the room. He did not have the strength to get up and pretend. He was consumed by insomnia and paranoia. He was too fragile for this world, too eager to help. So much so that he did not notice when he started disappearing.

On one fateful evening, just before his departure, he confided in me with a heavy heart, confessing that he felt as though he had usurped someone else's place in life. He spoke of his desire to depart suddenly, rather than fade into nothingness. He spoke of his yearning for Aniela, the girl he loved, and he lamented not having danced with her one last time next to a starry night, full of neon lights and Leonard Cohen's song "Dance Me to the End of Love". He told me of how he knew that she loved him more than anyone else, with her frequent morning, daytime, and even late-night calls, her voice charged with excitement, brimming with an impatient urgency to "listen! I must tell you something as soon as possible". He told me that he knew with that one sentence she has put him above everyone else. Because it was, he, not someone else, who was supposed to hear her stories of success and failure. It was him, not someone else who was supposed to hear her feelings, plans, panics, and drama. He would often tell me the world was too big for him when the truth was that the universe was too small for him. Black holes did not compare to the depth of his dark circles, and galaxies were the closest thing to the brightness of his eyes, his small moons. He was an ordinary boy, who enjoyed poetry and singing songs. But he despised the world, distrusted people, and perceived decay in everything around him. He abhorred falsehood and inconsistency and had become a boy without dreams.

"I just want tranquility, to do whatever I feel like doing anywhere, at any time, without having to think about excuses or justifications that then make me give up.", He told me in his sad voice on one of those nights when we would spend signing and talking on the fourth floor of our dormitory. He wanted to enjoy the sun on his face, the one that would announce the imminent arrival of Spring that is already in the air. He wanted to write, to be excited at once, without being influenced by anything or anyone. He wanted to listen to himself, give vent to his needs, even childish ones, and then return to being who he is.

I feel like people like him occur very rarely in life, if not at all, but when they do, they leave you with a measurable void. He was a poem full of beautiful metaphors in a world full of mediocre verses.

***

I spent the whole day being busy, calling, working, studying, reading, and running. Running like a wounded army commander, whose army is defeated despite victories. Then the night came, the silence and darkness prevailed, the former covered the world, and the latter covered the sky. I saw in front of me a beautiful girl, she looked just like you. She was swaying calmly to the rhythm of Chopin's Nocturne in B flat minor, Op. 9 no. 1; I saw myself dancing with her to the rhythm of her laughter and I was jovial. Like an eternity quickly passing by, I saw her in front of me and I saw nothing else after that. I looked for her as a soldier looking for his rifle on a battlefield!

Then I woke up. At first, I thought that it could not be a dream. Life cannot be that cruel. I prayed that this would be true. But the truth was only a blanket under my cheek and about 5 am in the morning on the clock. It was like showing a child a cute dog and letting him play with him. The child of unconsciousness will love a new friend, will play with him, and stroke his fur. And after a couple of hours, the parents will take the dog by the scruff of the neck and twist its neck right in front of the sobbing baby. From heaven to hell! I wanted to go to sleep just to have that dream again and never wake up. But I had another nightmare, and when I woke up, the nightmare began.

It is now a habit for me to think of you every night before going to sleep. I would complete my nightly dreams and then gently close my warm eyes and fall asleep. Last night, I wished we could have been together on a farm surrounded by wooden cottages. Where I would take your hand for a walk, and we would walk into the meadow next to the farm. We would watch the winds blow in the opposite direction to prevent us from reaching our destination. But you and I are beyond such trifles. Therefore, we would reach the middle of the meadow and lay down next to each other, you stare at the sky, and I would stare at you!

***

Dear Olena,

As I devoured each sentence of your letter, it was as though you stood before me once again. Your words were like sweet poison, intoxicating me with your tenderness and affection. And now, I declare to you without hesitation or ceremony, that I have fallen hopelessly in love with you. Never before have I felt such a desire for anyone, not even my own flesh and blood. How did it come to be? Only God knows. There is much that could be said, but why bother to praise you? You know my sincerity without requiring proof, my dear love. If ten tomes were written on this topic, they would be mere scratches on the surface. Why waste time with mere words of praise when the heart speaks a language far more powerful? There is no need to rationalize or justify what we feel, for it simply is.

The memories of those fleeting months spent with you in Wroclaw are etched into my soul like a work of art. The places we visited, each one filled with its own unique charm, the museums we explored, full of secrets and horrors, the churches we went to, with their looming, ominous architecture, the films we watched in the dimly lit cinema, the poems we penned and revised, the books and novels we dissected over tea and coffee. Yet, we had also endured great sufferings, and life had tested us harshly. And love, alluring love, like a delightful mirage, had tormented our thirsty souls. My thoughts are consumed with a desperate longing to see you once more, to feel your presence close to me again.

My words falter when I try to describe the depths of my feelings and attraction towards you, for they are dark and dangerous. And I am not one to spill my emotions so nakedly on a page, I swear, but in your presence, I am transparent. I am no master of words either, but there is no need for flowery language to express what we have shared in Wroclaw. But it is enough that you understand the depth of my obsession, my dear. You, of all people, know how tightly I was bound to you, how fiercely I loved you. It was not a love born of pure intentions or pure desires. It was a love that bordered on obsession, one that twisted and corrupted everything it touched. I am not proud of the person I was in the name of love, but I cannot deny its power over me.

The notion of soul mates and love at first sight, once dear to my heart, seems but mere illusions of the naïve. However, a growing sense of certainty begins to take hold within me, that perhaps in the course of one's life, one might stumble upon another who is perfectly suited to them. Not because they are perfect, or because you are, but because their flaws and yours are positioned in such a way that the two separate entities could merge, like two pieces of a puzzle, and finally complete a whole. Such was the verity of our love, I believe, that we were meant to be together, bound by our imperfections and united by our mutual longing for acceptance. And now, amidst the hush of the night, I hear the whispers of those who plead for their loved ones to return. But what do they truly expect? As for me, I cannot bring myself to ask for your return, for where you have gone, you have found solace in another's embrace, and who am I to shatter the peace you have found? How can I justify asking for your laughter to vanish once more? Regardless of where you find yourself on this vast earth, be it a distant land or a neighboring city, what matters is that you stand tall with that same captivating smile. The earth we share and the sky we look up to will always be the constant link that connects us.

***

The day I leave this world, find me in the flowers, find me in the moon and in the stars of the sky, find me in the sunflowers. Every time you need advice, look for me in the pages of books, because they know all my secrets.

When I leave, find me on the beach and high in the mountains. Find me in the movies, in music, and in the things I never said. Find me in my room, because only he heard my cries. Find me at night, in the dark sky, in the dark corner of the city.

The day I leave, find me in all the people I loved because I left a little of myself with them. Look for my friends from other places, and let them know that I miss them, that I have not forgotten them.

And when it rains, when you see the sky in pink; dance and laugh because I will be the one dancing and laughing with you. Always remember me in everything I said and wrote because only God and my writings know what I lived through.

***

Dear You,

Those two words, "Dear You," take me back to the time we wrote to each other after the night we first talked to each other at an evening gathering, held in our friend's apartment. The weather was pleasantly cold, our hearts were eager for each other, and our eyes were fixed on each other. Our encounter was a fascinating legend, a remedy for the restlessness of my heart. You spoke of your new apartment and roommates, and I told you about my new life in Wroclaw. Everyone around was having fun, talking, and laughing out loud. We, too, did not lag behind the masses. We saw each other with our eyes: mine was in love, and yours, I still did not understand. Your eyes were like Nalî's ghazals, your lips filled with dormant poems of Rumi, and each line of your face was an authentic epic from Shahnameh.

The weather is chilly at sunset over here, I lit the lights as an excuse to write a letter to you, but it did not diminish the melancholy of the room. I hope you understand that I always associate sunsets with the dream of being with you, otherwise, no solace can calm the sorrow that darkness brings. Glances through some old albums, I run my fingers over some photographs that are dear to me, begging to revive them at least one more time. But, in vain. That is not it. You cannot revive a living thing, which in your eyes has died a long time ago. We only sometimes, but sometimes, hid from the world, guarding each other's hands. We warmed our palms and released them slowly when they got thick. Looking back, I realize that I have been deceiving myself all my life back then. Every letter I wrote to you was a love letter. How could it have been any other way? Is there anything more romantic than someone handwriting you a love letter, slipping it between the pages of a book they recommended, to wait until you find it later? And I realize that all, but this one, were bad love letters. In those bad letters I asked you to reciprocate, but in this one, I ask nothing. I am happy to announce that this is my first good love letter to you. Because there is nothing more, I can do for you.

Today would be your birthday. I have written many letters to you, and I have hidden each one somewhere among my books, diaries, and phone notes. I know I have a letter somewhere, which I wrote to you two years ago, but I never had the courage to give it to you. Maybe it was better this way, for words are such small things in the face of all we owe each other. We owed each other some more laughter, some hugs between mutual wars, and a smile that would come out just by seeing you walk through the crowd. For your mere presence had the power to stop all the world wars in me. The knights would lay down their swords, the ladies would stop playing their deadly games, the children would fall asleep with a sweet dream, and the old people would cast off their anxiety. The whole world would freeze inside me just by seeing you coming from afar. And by then, I would no longer be in need of art, music, or literature because you would become my art, music, and literature.

Do you remember when I once told you that life revolves around the rule of reason and that anything that goes against that rule ruins life? It has been a long time since I have been doing things that not only are not rational but are pure madness. I had heard that the heart can take a person somewhere that the mind never imagined, but I had never thought that this could happen to me. For several weeks I have been thinking at what exact moment I realized that I love you. And I sit again, and again, thinking, and I cannot remember exactly when this realization came to me, and I believe that this is love after all.

***

Nuremberg, October 13, 2020

As of late, I have slowly become a ghost. A gray, translucent shadow of the past - with dreams in the heart, burning eyes, and a soul that subtly feels the world around. My soul resembles an old, empty house, haunted by ghosts of my past. They wander the darkened corridors, lost in mourning for the dead illusions and expectations that once filled these rooms. Their mournful eyes gaze out of the windows, longing to return to the world they once knew, but to which they will never return. I cried to the sky and to the moon on most nights because I did not do anything wrong to deserve this cruel eternal rejection. I hugged myself from the humid early morning wind, while my lungs were hurt by their allergic condition. It did not matter! Nothing hurt more than seeing the mirror of my impoverished and scourged soul. There was no need to look for reasons, I understood that some were born to receive everything life offered, and I was that orphan, it was part of the balance.

I swallowed the tears inside my tangled chest, accepting gracefully: "Okay. If you wish, I will dedicate myself to serving and giving, but I will never be deluded, because I know my end in each farewell." I smiled, despite the stab wounds to my soul, my red eyes, and my broken voice, and started looking at old photographs of everyday life that I took, listening to playlists and my old guitar playing, reviewing my collection of books, and reading my diary. Here is a memory of Dylan and I sitting on the fourth-floor corridor of our dormitory, playing our guitars, and singing Leonard Cohen's song "One of us cannot be wrong". Here is the record of an interesting conversation I had with a German man at Café Księgarnia Tajne Komplety, enjoying listening to his life story of finding his love, and now his wife, in Wroclaw. Here is a copy of Milan Kundera's book "The Unbearable Lightness of Being" which Olena gave me the day we met at Garden Café.

But the nightmare returns one more time. I put my hands on my forehead, bulging my eyes. My chest rises often and unevenly. The demon within is aware of my presence, eager to escape. A hot, sticky drool oozes out of his mouth, burning through my innards. The fangs are furiously trying to pierce and suck the remnants of strength and emotions out of me. I want to ride in pain and crush everything, longing to disappear from every corner and never return in life or in the next. But...This cannot be. I bring my hands to my chest, holding everything like I am trying to stop the beast inside. I close my eyes, attempting to calm myself a bit. For the first time in a very long time, I am unable to summon my thoughts, even after reading two books in the last month. I feel like they all ran around corners, afraid of responsibility. After all, with their help, I try to accomplish the impossible - to turn into a verbal form of the raging ocean of Ivan Aivazovsky's painting, the Ninth Wave.

All of a sudden, I want to talk about white butterflies, painted in pink houses. About sweet wisteria and bees bearing mourning. I long to delve into the world of faceless men, those stripped of their desires, the tombstone trees, the lonely señor, about the river that will turn the village into a bloody wave. I desire to dwell on a girl who stood up in the center of a dead sundial instead of a gnome and read from her poem, "What difference what time it is? Time is you and me". I still love bright penetrating images of hers, my heart beats in the rhythm of her text. I still feel that unbearable sadness about the part of the man who lives in the book side by side with unimaginable beings.

I see the world differently. The world is fraught with beautiful and ugly, sublime, and low, kind and terrible, and we absorb the manifestations of each category by bit, melting them and molding them into the unique patterns of our souls. Only those we are ready to let in will eventually get along inside us. Looking inside myself, I see this wild, chaotic, bizarrely intertwined pile of things, impressions of memories, invented characters, places, lubricated sensations, scraps read somewhere, and once phrases, snakes of dreams. The people who appeared and loved in different periods of my life are similar to the architectural extensions that are different in styles added to the skeleton of the ancient building. I have found that people are fond of talking. They chatter endlessly, their words echoing off the stone walls. But I have never been one for idle chatter. I carry on an inner monologue, but the words seldom leave my lips. My thoughts and emotions swirl inside me like storms, but the words rarely find their way out. I refuse to believe that I am a mess, as they may think. I am just a deeply feeling person in a messy world. For that when others ask me why I cry so often, I simply tell them the truth: "For the same reason I laugh so often… because I am paying attention."

***

This usually happens at the beginning of September: suddenly a strong warm wind sweeps down from the mountains, carrying with it the last remnants of summer, it fills the city streets with the scent of mountain herbs and flowers, a haunting reminder of the season that is slowly slipping away. People look at each other with surprise in the first minutes and ask, "What is it?" What is this warm wind from the gorge? But then, the memory comes to their aid: have you forgotten how summer is leaving? It is the mountains that send you their last summer greetings before they cover themselves with snow. This is the summer wind trying to gently hug you for the last time this year. And for some reason, people's faces become sad. They rush to burn the garbage before the autumn rains come. And the smell of smoke joins the aroma of flowers. Bit by bit, he pushes summer out of the city, and autumn claims its rights: now this place belongs to me. The next morning, people wake up in a dark, cool room. The wind no longer blows, and the blue sky is covered with a gray veil of clouds. When people venture outside to work, they dress warmly and carry umbrellas: summer is finally gone, and you never know what to expect from autumn.

The time is finally approaching for heavy rains and the bewitching leaf falls, which means that it is time for me to hide in a blanket, arm myself with something warm and fragrant and make a list of autumn books that can make dank evenings even more atmospheric. It is another September day. You understand that today is the best time to get your coat. While the elements are raging over Nuremberg, a lull has come into my soul. It has been raining all day, but after the autumn rain the streets are deserted and quiet, so I am planning to put on my coat and go for quiet walks in the park, listening to the rustle of yellow leaves after the rain. The main thing is not to get caught in a sudden downpour. This is probably why I love Autumn, its aesthetics, the very atmosphere. We are similar. The same inconstancy, melancholy. Can you smell autumn with the aroma of pine, wet earth, and fallen leaves? weather like this makes you want to jump out of your cold office and take the tram back to a mansion on the edge of town. Open the door, take a deep breath, and hum to yourself in profound contentment "I'm at home."

Even on the warmest and sunniest day, I will always prefer rain and a cold nose. I look forward to long quiet walks through deserted parks, thinking about the history of this place and imagining that I live in the Middle Ages, walking early in the morning along an empty street, hiding my face in a scarf from the icy wind, doing my homework under the light of candles, spending recess talking with the librarian, tangling in millions of notebooks and textbooks, drinking hot ginger tea, warming my hands in the sleeves of a black wool sweater. I love autumn for it resonates with my innermost need for melancholy and sadness, for there is a certain poetry in the demise of the year, an air of mystery too. Lately, with bated breath, I have a wild desire to walk around the city and its deserted parks. One. Just me, music in headphones, and autumn.

***

Nuremberg, January 6, 2021

I am always amazed by this incredible, divine trait in people - the need to create. The desire to embody invisible images that ripen in the mind, to give physical embodiment to unseeable fantasies and ideas. To breathe life into the imagination. This is the same power that languished in Michelangelo's fingers when he cut lifeless pieces from cold marble, the same energy seething in the hands of Beethoven, ordering the notes in the Moonlight Sonata. This is the same sparkling power that moved Dostoevsky's pen.

This craving for beauty appeared at the dawn of history, as the human heart trembled from the sky covered with ripe stars and clouds. The eyes absorbed the magic of the sky blooming with sunrises and sunsets, and the soul was excited by the ringing bird trills and the murmur of crystal waters. Not yet able to compose sounds into words, people already tried to reproduce the beauty of the world around them. The human spirit has generated a myriad of poems, sculptures, and paintings, trying to piece together a portrait of an overwhelming, heartrending concept, the desire for which is the cornerstone, a stone laid in the very being of man. Is not this passionate need to surround yourself with beauty, to plunge into its maelstrom, dissolving into atoms, the highest degree of art worshiping?

She lives from the very first drawing drawn by primitive people in dark rocky valleys, constantly changing and changing appearances. She lives immortal and bestows immortality on those who receive her. Sometimes it seems to me that I live only to get lost in the pages, twist an unlit cigarette in my hands, and brew mint tea. Drowning in other people's eyes-lives-destinies, wrapping myself in a huge plaid shirt that has long become a part of me. It seems that I live only to look for something dear and half-forgotten in this world, and if not finding it, to wander on, protecting the smoldering ember of hope – otherwise, why live? My greatest fear, I think, is the demise of imagination. When the world outside is reduced to mere shades of pink and black rooftops - captured by a photographic mind that conveys truth, but a meaningless truth.

It is for the power of synthesis, the ability to shape and mold new worlds, that I crave. It is only for this that I dedicate myself to the task of seeking out this beauty, determined to leave no stone unturned. Nothing will be safe from my keen eyes and ears as I pursue this quest in the world for any trace of beauty that I could find. I still want to write something poetically beautiful about seasons, about music, about love, about the blue sky above my head and the fresh wind through the window, about the singing of birds, about my feelings on those wonderful days but in the end, all this remains settled on the lips with unspoken phrases. They bloom in my smiles, shine in my eyes, and splash out into the world with awkward dance steps on empty streets. I am torn between two feelings, and I do not understand - unsure whether to keep my joy to myself with a silent smile or to burst out in laughter for all to hear.

***

In literature, we are expected to know how to understand the meaning invested by the author in the work. We are expected to look for hidden milestones by which the writer brings us to the point. I like to believe that literature has a purpose beyond mere entertainment, for it brings sense to an otherwise senseless world. This is a noble pursuit, this is the purpose of literature - one that allows us to exchange experiences, impressions, and knowledge, to have dialogue that spans generations and continents. Literature is not a mere allegory. It is a visceral journey into another world, a world that you must enter fully and completely. You must breathe in the same air as the characters, feel what they feel, think what they think, and become utterly involved in their fate. Without this total immersion, you cannot hope to empathize with them. And it is this empathy that breathes life into literature.

Yet, it is equally important to recognize which aspects of a book speak to us the most. What draws us in, what captures our attention? Perhaps the author only briefly described something, trying to dilute the narrative with minor details, but it is these penetrating touches that could become the cherished moments in the book, fondly remembered above all others. After all, a lively dialogue does not occur according to the planned algorithm, it takes twists and turns that no one could anticipate, the interlocutors constantly jump from one topic to another, treading new paths in the dark thicket of the discussion. So, the book, telling us about one thing, can lead to completely new questions and reasoning, creating a new branch of the conversation. This is how the dialogue evolves, thrives, and spreads, flowing like a ship adrift in space-time, painting the indifferent cosmos with its unyielding radiance.

I do not think I know more about life than anyone my age, but it seems to me that a book is more reliable as a conversational partner than a friend or a lover. A novel or a poem is not a monologue, but a conversation between a writer and a reader—a conversation, I repeat, extremely private, excluding everyone else, mutually antisocial, if you like. During this conversation, the writer is equal to the reader, regardless of whether he is a great writer or not. I tend to wholeheartedly believe that no reader is average. The mere fact that they embark on reading and actually read already sets them apart in today's times. This equality is the equality of consciousness, and it stays with the reader for life in the form of a memory, vague or distinct. And sooner or later, by the way, or inopportunely, determines the behavior of the individual. This is what I mean when I speak of the role of the performer, which is only natural since a novel or a poem is the product of the mutual loneliness of the writer and reader.

***

Wrocław, January 14, 2021

I am sitting on a bench in the park near my dormitory, and while I inattentively watch trees longing for spring and a clear sky, I get lost in thoughts that hover in my turbulent mind. And so, I start thinking about the day I am facing, those already faced, and those I will face. I think of the words said and those avoided for fear of hurting, or simply due to excessive shyness, and to those that I would like to shout to silence my heart; to the complexities of life, to what good I have done, to what I have not done, and to what there is to do which unfortunately or fortunately is still so much. Decades of thoughts circled in my head. Lost in a sea of sighs, I now only dream of letting myself be carried away, swept by the current, getting caught in the whirl, and embarking on a journey to the north. To reach the harbor. To do nothing but spin in a sea full of life. To perceive meaning. I need a cup of coffee. an excellent therapist, some wise old human to cry to. A poem that will have my neck between its teeth. I need to go somewhere far. To retreat, to overcome my fear of trying and of facing a blank page.

My wild thoughts shift from the wide sky to the rushing people who ran almost blindly, losing everything, leaving behind memories, joys, and hope. I realize they cannot see each other. Lost in everyday life, pressed by the pressure of time, do not notice small but beautiful events. They miss their relationships and chances at love, which is supposed to be the foundation of good. Maybe they are afraid of love, therefore, run from her. Hiding and unable to speak, they are sinking into the abyss of nonsense. They could no longer appreciate the little things, or enjoy the music, tastes, and smells. The pursuit of wealth fell like a heavy axe on their already tired eyes. I see it but I cannot change it. I think about what I can do to make people rediscover joy and peace, to start talking to each other, to stop being afraid, and to be able to take risks for something beautiful. How can I get people to stop denying their feelings and be able to own them by articulating them out loud?

And suddenly my attention is captured by a little girl who, while walking, looks at me giving me a beautiful smile, one of those that only children know how to give, making even the eyes smile. A contagious smile that you cannot help but reciprocate. And it is in that moment that the world stops for a moment to make room for enchantment and joy, without anything else being frightening anymore. Humming in my thoughts "Birds on the Wire", taking a deep breath that would flood my lungs, filling them with icy waves, and thinking about you for one last time with a smile!

***

No one knew how to carry sadness as elegantly as she did with grace. As if it was a priceless piece of jewelry that she wore around her neck. She had long accepted the fact that she lived in a cruel world. The lady, who was chaos personified, could only be seen as such by a select few in her eyes. The lady whose touch could make your body tremble, the lady whose laugh could fill the room. The lady you would stand in silence next to and hope she would notice you because you did not dare to approach her. You would secretly admire her. She would never look straight into the eyes, she never allowed anyone to look into her soul. She felt everything too deeply as if the weight of the world were too much for her fragile heart. She might have had a lot to handle, but she was a lot to lose, too. She was a favorite of stray cats. They would come and warm their skinny sides on her knees while she was immersed herself in the plots of tattered books, sitting on a bench.

I was one of the lucky chosen ones that she let close enough to understand she could only give so much love because she never had it herself. She once loved me, a burnt-out old soul whose only offering was the weight of my own pain. Me, who wanted to leave this world, but stayed only until I met her.

She was a marvel of kindness, gentle and surprising, her spirit light and cheerful, yet somehow weary. Her outer life was not desolate, for none were worshiped as much as she was. Yet, within her, a desolation dwelled so profound that it filled even me with fear. Her very being seemed to emanate a haunting aura of emptiness, an abyss that I could not fathom nor comprehend. In her presence, I was overcome with a sense of solemn introspection, as if peering into the depths of my own soul. She often looked sad. Too young yet so old in her soul. Tired of life, as if in her attempt to catch the sun, she got lost in the mist. She loved watching the raging ocean. Sometimes she would smile at the thought that it was too similar to what was going on inside her. A storm. She looked so calm, almost indifferent to the world, while so much was raging in her soul. Yet, she was a genius in her quietness, able to immerse herself perfectly in that world.

She was a poetic, charming girl, overflowing with life! And with a smile like her, she could distract any devil, too. She could make any devil love her like a devoted saint. I knew there was something about her, something which I did not understand. For in her world of quietness, her eyes glittered like splintered glass in the sunlight. Sometimes I felt like her eyes changed color with her mood. They were heavenly blue when she was happy and free, turned turquoise when she was angry, and shimmered in violet when she was very sad. And it was through those eye gazes, I could see her heart, too. A velvet, soft heart she had, as gentle as a whisper. And yet when she was speaking, her voice was like liquid gold, so calming, healing every cell in my body.

I wish I could still call her and hear her voice. But her voice has become a poisonous chalice that burns my heart. Thoughts and dreams of her bring a sorrow deeper than the ocean and my love for her does not die the way hers had died for me. The more

I love her a little more than yesterday, the further I find out that her love has been deeper than an ocean and wider than the sky. It shows me how little I felt of her love all those times and how much darkness I was exposed to until I found her.

***

Life can be an enigma, an intricate puzzle whose pieces stubbornly refuse to fit, a maze whose walls persistently keep me trapped, leaving me lost and bewildered. As a writer, my pen becomes my sword, cutting through the thicket of confusion and carving a path toward clarity. Each stroke is a deliberate strike, aimed at finding meaning in the chaos, a light in the darkness. But there are moments when the forest grows dense and impenetrable, and my pen falls silent, unable to cut through the tangle of my own thoughts and emotions. It is in these moments that I turn to nature, seeking solace in the delicate beauty of a wildflower, a symbol of hope and resilience in a world that often feels too challenging to comprehend.

I have sat down many times in terror and dread writing tales of lives and realities I have no personal experience of, I have been hesitant to share those stories with others, fearing the kind of harsh judgment that society so easily dishes out. Yet when I do not write, I feel like a wandering ghost aimlessly floating through the sea of my own thoughts. It therefore feels refreshing to return to writing after some time, it is such a surge of nostalgia, memories, sensations, and awe. I consider it a full-fledged diary of thoughts when I look through my memories, flip through my old records and past texts, and the words begin to flow once again. I remember the details that have already been erased from my memory, I see my past through new eyes, my memories like old photographs that have been left to gather dust, and this is both overwhelming and melancholy. It is sad that all of them are left in the past and the impossibility of them happening is certain, but they will always be mine, nonetheless.

Time is such a perplexing reality. It does not always flow in the same way, there are days so thoughtful, but so heavy that you carry them with you even when they are long gone. That time keeps flowing inside you even if it no longer flows outside. It feels strange to think about how a year that started in one way can end in a completely opposite way. It feels strange because often we think that things will last forever, that a familiar situation should last forever just because we have grown accustomed to it. And yet, things can change in just one day, and what was once so familiar starts to slip away, until you do not even recognize its shadow anymore.

Looking back, I see some people left here; others came back. Someone died, and someone is born. And this is wonderful, this is the dynamics of life, the cycle. Maybe someone will come back later.

***

Wrocław, 2022

I wake up to the sound of rain on the window. It has been raining all night and the forecast said it would continue all day. I lazily get out of bed, not wanting to face the cold and damp outside. I brew some coffee, and in a cup, I search for a taste that is inspiring, a beautiful conviction that will illuminate my imagination. I become the captain, the sailor, the ship as I play Frédéric Chopin's piece - "Raindrop" Prelude and immerse myself in the sounds of piano echoing through the apartment. The rain continues to strike against the windows and sills. It is getting darker. And suddenly I hear thunder, everything goes dark. The music stops, and I stand in the middle of the room. In silence, mixed with the aroma of coffee. I suddenly asked myself "Why is it that people often forget that artists themselves are works of art too?"

Those who possess the ability to appreciate everything and everyone around them with mere words, a splash of color, a rhythmic arrangement of melody, or a simple click of their camera, are deserving of appreciation themselves. How many times have poets yearned to become the very words of someone else's poetry? How many times have painters longed to be captured on canvas? They lay their souls bare for the world to mock, they pour their heart and soul into their craft, with the same unwavering passion and love as always. Oh, the marvels of creative souls! The artists, writers, poets, sculptors, and all those gifted beings, are nothing short of miraculous. It is a wonder to witness the sheer power of their imagination as they transform wild ideas, untamed emotions, and feelings that thrive within the depths of their consciousness. To think that these creatures can so effortlessly breathe life into their innermost musings, leaving us in awe and wonderment, is enough to make my heart melt.

At times, I cannot help but wish that I could visit the forgotten artists of the past, those who were never appreciated for their individual selves, but rather only for the things they created. I wish I could knock on their doors and say, "I am working on something. Would you like to be my muse?" I wish I could converse with them about their art and watch their eyes light up as they discuss their creations. It sounds beautiful, is not it? Because it helps to lose oneself. The best thing about this kind of creativity is the moment when you dissolve in it. You forget who you are and where you are. There is no you, no problems, not even thoughts. The pen itself writes out the words and puts them into lines. To be someone's writing, to be addressed with your name and all those other affectionate words too in someone's poem.

***

Hey. I am not really great with introductions, but here I am. My name is... well... I do not remember. They call me Mute, an account of I do not speak much if at all, I guess. They think there is something wrong with me. They talk about me like I am not real, or like I am a ghost. I can hear them whisper. I can hear their laughs and see their grins. I am not stupid. I just do not have much to say.

So, as you can guess, I do not really have any friends. There is this older lady that lives two doors down from me, I call her Rita. She is nice. Sometimes I mow her lawn or pick the weeds from her garden. In return, she will give me these notepads or paint or sketchbooks. She says I remind her of her estranged son. He used to write for her all the time and draw her pictures for her walls. She hates them being bare. She says it makes her feel lonely. So, I guess you could say Rita is my friend. Because without my work, she would be lonely, and without her gifts, I would be...... Empty.

***

Wroclaw, March 19, 2022

It was not as easy as you think it was, it became easier after a hundred fights I went through in my head, a thousand shattered pieces of my broken heart which I had to pick here and there, sleepless nights spent drowning in a sea of tears. Even as they wander down their own paths, these long conversations, scattered thoughts, and unspoken longings, like creatures from the depths of the sea, brought up to the surface, their voices still find me in a gentle whisper "Are you asleep?" at night. So yes, processing all my life experiences was not as easy as you think it was. It required me to eat up all my feelings at once, leaving me only with this cold, lifeless shell of a person that you see. I am aware that these are not easy texts. Sometimes intricate, overly complicated, perhaps even incomprehensible. However, I hope that those of you who read them are not tired or mentally drained. I really would not want that. I also do not want to write nonsense, gibberish, because although it happens to me sometimes, I have reached a certain age and I have to pretend to be an adult, serious, and composed person.

You do not really understand, I do not tremble at the prospect of failing, nor I am afraid of putting in wasted efforts. It matters little if I never achieve anything in life. What scares me the most is the sudden vanishment of passion, the sudden disappearance of my interest in life. It is to one day wake up to the world, finding out the fire in my heart has gone forever like a wind, and that the things that once brought me boundless joy and euphoria have now abandoned me, leaving me in a state of numbness. But do you understand what this means to a heart like mine? To see the glow of desire and passion fading away like a burning candle at its end! And that when I look at things around me, I feel nothing! As if there is an absolute emptiness inside toward everything outside. I am not worried about what people think of me, for my world exists solely within my own mind. I wage my battles within the confines of my thoughts, in a realm that belongs to me and me alone. But if one day by any chance you saw me soulless like an abandoned stove, then you must know that day meant the end of life to me.

And honest to God, I was trying to fade into the void, to crumble into nothingness. I pleaded to hear nothing, to see nothing, to feel nothing, to speak of nothing. But as if I was born a crime, I feel everything now. I stumbled upon an ocean inside my chest, and the ship of my being is sinking in it, and it keeps wanting to leak through my eyes. Such has been my crime ever since I was a child. I wanted nothing for myself but the clear blue sky, the sunlight, and the cool breeze in the moonlight. I wanted the climax of non-attachment, where one is entirely sufficient to oneself. For years, I kept quiet. I only talked to people I trusted, and there were not many of them. I preferred to spend time in my own world. And although I really value the people around me, I prefer to pour my thoughts on paper and put them in a drawer, so that in a few years I can burn with shame and let them burn along with my tears. I have taken shelter in that part of me that does not love anyone anymore and I will remain there forever. Yet, I still like to listen to people's problems, worries, pains, and sorrows. Sitting patiently as I listen, lending a helping hand where I can.

I walk back and forth within myself; I am quite used to being alone. The four walls of my room have kept me more company than all the people around me. I am not afraid of retreating to secluded areas where I can loudly ache in peace with no one around to watch and laugh, uninterrupted and at peace, hoping that this loneliness I crave could finally heal me in ways no one else could. To me, this feeling of loneliness is divine, it is the pull of the soul toward its origin, to merge back into the Divine. I drown in the loneliness of being, without being saved by anything or anyone except the Divine. For years, all I expected was this; the feeling of being understood without having to go through the pain of having to explain. Yet I find myself often required to explain and it crushes me over and over in the midst of tragedies, to the point I sometimes begin to outline life with a phrase similar to Vincent Van Gogh's final words, "the sadness will last forever." Yet this ecstasy of the Divine's love I feel in my heart is prevailing beyond any words, understandings, and languages, and the spirit is perceiving a great symphony where strings are being played by something divine.

Amidst all these passing moments, I can assure everyone that I am happy. It is not a lie, I promise you. I am happy. Nonetheless, let it be known to you that this happiness does not shield me from relapses. Some days, when self-doubt grips me, it becomes so difficult that my mind becomes a murky blur, and I cannot tell white from black. Sometimes, my world gets cold with loneliness, and I convince myself that I cannot ever rightly "fit in". Some nights, I do long for the touch of another, someone who can reassure me that I am okay and if I am not, I will be. Some days, I just need a kind reminder that I am not what I am going through;

I am not the sum of my broken parts; and I am much more than what I make myself out to be.

My love language is loyalty, regardless of the weather, regardless of whether you shine today or dark tomorrow. I cling to the hope that I can leave a good mark on the lives of those around me. I hope that the footsteps I leave behind will not be washed away by the sands of time. That memories of me will create ripples that continue to spread long after I am gone. That when they remember me, they will say, "Once there was this guy who did not cause me hurt with his words, who has not made fun of my grief, who did not leave me alone in the middle of my battle with depression and sadness, and when I was lost in my life, he was always waiting for me with his open arms".

Because I believe at the end of this path which we call life, we are all going to become stories. I hope I am a beautiful story in your life. One that you can tell people around you and they smile. For I have suffered a lot from people who walked into my life just to leave their arrows in my heart and watch how I suffer. Familiar faces who left me to my pains, to battle my demons alone, to face my own brokenness.

***